Eco-innovation and Sustainability Management

Sustainability is a phenomenon that must be pursued in a complex system of interrelated elements of business, society and ecology. It is important to gain an understanding of these elements, the interplay among them and the behavior of the system. This book explores the business-societal-and-ecological system in which sustainable innovation has to be envisioned, conceptualized, realized and improved. Author Bart Bossink offers insight into the systematic coherence of drivers of eco-innovation and sustainability utilizing a three-part approach: (1) eco- and sustainable innovation in business is based on ideas and people who cooperatively develop these ideas; (2) groups of people, organized in commercial firms, must realize these ideas cooperatively and create the innovations that can conquer the market; and (3) people from governmental, nongovernmental, not-for-profit, research and commercial organizations can build institutional arrangements that stimulate these sustainable innovations, changing both industry and society.

Adopting a managerial perspective and discussing concepts and methods to manage eco-innovation and sustainability in business, this book highlights the interrelated roles of the individual, the firm, partnerships and business environments. Researchers and practitioners who want to combine a commercial and economical approach with an ethical and social ambition to create an ecologically sustainable firm stand to learn much from these pages.

Bart Bossink is professor of technology and innovation at the Faculty of Economic Sciences and Business Administration and at the Faculty of Natural Sciences of VU University Amsterdam in the Netherlands. He obtained a master's degree in industrial engineering and management and a Ph.D. in civil engineering and management from the University of Twente. He has more than twenty years of research experience in the field of eco-innovation and sustainability management. Numerous papers of his have been published as articles in various scientific and professional journals. One of his books was nominated for best management book of the year in Belgium. In 2008 he received the outstanding paper award from the Emerald Literati Network. His research is acknowledged and supported by both governmental and commercial organizations, resulting in financial support, tight cooperation in research projects, and lectures and workshops for practitioners.

Routledge Studies in Innovation, Organization and Technology

Eco-innovation and Sustainability Management

Bart Bossink

Routledge
Taylor & Francis Group
New York London

First published 2012
by Routledge
711 Third Avenue, New York, NY 10017

Simultaneously published in the UK
by Routledge
2 Park Square, Milton Park, Abingdon, Oxon OX14 4RN

First issued in paperback 2017

*Routledge is an imprint of the Taylor & Francis Group,
an informa business*

Library of Congress Cataloging-in-Publication Data

Bossink, Bart, 1967–
    Eco-innovation and sustainability management / by Bart Bossink.
        p. cm. — (Routledge studies in innovation, organization
        and technology ; 21)
    Includes bibliographical references and index.
    1. Management—Environmental aspects.   2. Technological
innovations—Environmental aspects.   3. Technological innovations—
Economic aspects.   4. Sustainable development.   I. Title.
    HD30.255.B67   2012
    658.4'083—dc23
    2012036202

ISBN 13: 978-1-138-10795-3 (pbk)
ISBN 13: 978-0-415-81872-8 (hbk)

Typeset in Sabon
by Apex CoVantage, LLC

Contents

Figures

Tables

Foreword

Each year, in my graduate classes I ask young and bright business and science students: "What will you choose when you get a car for free? Imagine you get it from me. What would you choose? A gasoline car of a premium brand with high CO_2 emissions or a hybrid car of a less fancy brand but with an electric motor with significantly lower CO_2 emissions?" The past three years, the outcome has always been the same: 75 percent chose the premium air polluter. Yes, the next generation chooses the unsustainable option. Each year I then start a conversation about the students' motivations, and their main reason is always the same. It is: "Premium brand! Premium brand! Premium brand!" Every year I then immediately change the experiment. I offer them two almost identical versions of the same premium-brand car and ask them again: "What will you choose when you get the premium-brand car for free? Imagine you will get it from me. What would you choose? A gasoline-powered, unsustainable version or a hybrid, more sustainable version?" Fifty percent still choose the unsustainable version. Yes, these youngsters are less innovation-minded than I thought. "Why?" I ask them repeatedly. "Because of the nice sound of a combustion engine. . . . Because I am used to gasoline cars. . . . Because, what happens when the battery of that eco-car fails?" These conversations do not confuse me anymore. Over the past twenty years I have gotten used to these or similar kinds of interactions. I have, for example, gotten used to the many different points of view that come up when the sustainability issue is discussed. Positions vary from "nonsense: you can't eat sustainability" to "people-planet-profit" to "we must go back to our natural position on the planet and listen to Mother Earth." Even people, who agree that humanity has to become eco-innovative and sustainable can disagree on how to pursue this goal. Some think we have to inform the consumer. Others say that we have to punish polluters and reward the best of class. A third group wants to change national policy and regulation. A fourth group wants to subsidize sustainable initiatives. Another group states that we do not have to do anything and can simply rely on eco-innovative start-up firms that will generate a completely new sustainable industry and society. More than once, I was in the middle of discussions between representatives of these groups, discussions that sometimes ended up in some kind of trench warfare, where everybody stuck to his or her own opinion and was trying to convince the other; with a lot of talking and not so much listening. As long as people do not hurt each other and as long as each group tries to realize sustainability according to its own ideas, I think that is okay. However, I think we can do better. I even think that all these people are right at the same time, that trench warfare is not necessary and that all these opinions and approaches can be merged in a systematic and coherent approach.

Since sustainability is a phenomenon that has to be pursued in a complex business-societal-and-ecological system that consists of interrelated elements, it is important to gain an understanding of the elements that make up the system, of the interplay among the elements and of the behavior of the system. It is thus of importance to know what the elements of the system are and how these relate to one another. Therefore, this book explores the business-societal-and-ecological system in which sustainable innovation has to be envisioned, conceptualized, realized and improved. It can be of interest to scholars, students and practitioners who want to gain an insight into the systematic coherence of drivers of eco-innovation and sustainability in business, industry and society. The main concepts of the book are that (1) eco- and sustainable innovation in business is based on ideas and people who cooperatively develop these ideas; (2) groups of people, organized in commercial firms, realize these ideas cooperatively and create the innovations that can conquer the market; and (3) people from governmental, nongovernmental, not-for-profit, research and commercial organizations can build institutional arrangements that stimulate these sustainable innovations to grow large and thereby change industry and society.

In the coming years, unsustainable firms can make way for transparent, clean and value-conscious firms, for eco-innovative and sustainable firms, firms that deliver value to shareholders and stakeholders, that satisfy personal and societal needs, and that care for and support people, animals and the green and blue environment. In the coming time, profitable business models can be those business models that are dedicated to profit in a much broader sense; the broader sense of private and public well-being, health and prosperity. Viable, sustainable businesses of the future can be the ones that grow naturally, serve humanely, provide shelter and care for life and the living. These businesses can have a well-meant respect for and gratitude to planet Earth. The future sustainable industrial landscape can be a landscape of tightly cooperating organizations that concentrate on a fair distribution of production and consumption among people and on continuous reuse and reprocessing of materials and energy resources—a motivating vision, I think. I hope this book will contribute to the realization of this vision.

This book could not have been realized without the support I got from Routledge and VU University Amsterdam. In particular, I thank Deepti Agarwal, Terry Clague, Jerilyn Famighetti, Stacy Noto, Laura Stearns, Lauren Verity and Jonas Voorzanger for their invaluable support, friendly advice, kind answers to my e-mails and results-oriented handling of the manuscript.

Bart Bossink

1 Eco-innovation and Sustainability

1.1 INTRODUCTION

This book presents a model of eco-innovation and sustainability management. To researchers this model provides a coherent overview of the main elements of the eco-innovation and sustainability management system. It proposes, evaluates and discusses relationships among these elements. The model helps managers to decide which actions to take to develop eco-innovation and sustainability in commercial firms, not-for-profit organizations, nongovernmental organizations and governmental organizations.

This book defines eco-innovation and sustainability management as the development of new initiatives in an organization to sustain, improve and renew the environmental, social and societal quality of its business processes and the products and services these business processes produce. In this definition, the measures and targets of environmental, social and societal quality can have various dimensions, such as reduced pollution and limited use of natural resources; the provision of services not just to shareholders but to all stakeholders of the organization; and contributions to societal problems, including employment for the disabled and education for the untrained. In this book, the "sustainability" concept covers this broad array of issues.

The model in this book introduces three basic managerial levels for eco-innovation and sustainability: co-ideation, co-innovation and co-institutionalization. Co-ideation is defined as the cooperation of individuals who want to generate, develop and disseminate new sustainable thoughts, concepts, plans and suggestions for business. Co-innovation is defined as the cooperation of individuals who are situated in commercial organizations and who want to transform new sustainable thoughts, concepts, plans and suggestions for business into new viable, profitable and working business proposals in industry. Co-institutionalization is defined as the cooperation of individuals who are situated in commercial, not-for-profit, nongovernmental and governmental organizations and who want to create structural stimuli and arrangements that enable these new viable, profitable and working business proposals to become important in industry. The three managerial levels serve as the framework for the theory-building studies in this book. This book addresses questions such as these: What can personal leadership do for eco-innovation and sustainability? What is the role of entrepreneurs who invest and believe in eco-innovation and sustainability? What exactly can champions, that is, the persons who walk and talk innovation all the time, do for eco-innovation and sustainability? The studies in this book also elaborate on the contributions of teams, the functions of projects and project management, the embedding of teams and projects in firms and cooperation and partnerships among commercial firms, not-for-profit organizations, nongovernmental organizations and governmental organizations. It explores what these different forms of organization can do to improve ecological, social and societal quality. Finally, this book delves into the opportunities for people and organizations to institutionalize sustainable knowledge, revenues and achievements and create a powerful and large business that is eco-innovative and sustainable. It deals with the impact of markets, clients, customers, societal pressure groups, scientific and technological progress, and national policy and regulation.

This introductory chapter presents the three basic managerial levels of the model of eco-innovation and sustainability management (Section 1.2). It describes the methodology that is used to develop and build this model (Section 1.3). It compares the model with two other established models in the literature to put the characteristics into a broader theoretical perspective (Section 1.4). It concludes with a brief summary (Section 1.5).

1.2   THE ECO-INNOVATION AND SUSTAINABILITY MODEL

As stated in the introduction, this section introduces the three basic levels at which eco-innovation and sustainability management take place. The three levels are co-ideation, co-innovation and co-institutionalization. Cooperation is a key concept at all three levels. Co-ideation stands for all cooperative action of individuals to develop ideas with innovation potential in sustainability and that can be translated into effective solutions for business. Co-innovation is the cooperative activity of individuals in organizations to actually translate the ideas and solutions that originated at the co-ideation level into profitable businesses. Co-institutionalization is the cooperative effort of public and private parties to integrate the successful sustainable business proposals and businesses into the institutional environment and let the new emerging sustainable businesses grow into mature and widespread businesses with a large impact on industry and society.

The first of three starting points of this book is that eco- and sustainable innovation can be conceptualized as a linear process. The co-ideation level for eco-innovation and sustainability can be perceived as the start of the innovation process and that is followed by co-innovation and completed with co-institutionalization. Second, at the same time, this linear process can also be seen as cyclical, in the sense that the linear process goes on continuously,

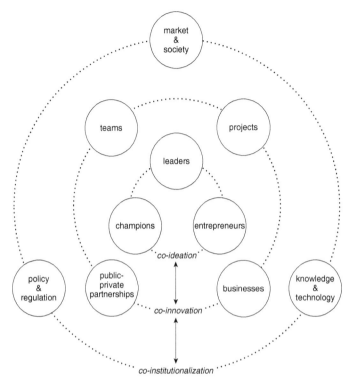

Figure 1.1   The eco-innovation and sustainability system.

repeats itself over and over again and by this is a main driver of sustainable innovation and continuous improvement in organizations and society. Third, the eco- and sustainable innovation process can also be seen as interdependent, interactive and transformative, which means that aspects or elements of the different levels influence one another continuously. It implies that co-ideation drives co-innovation and co-innovation drives co-institutionalization but also that, in addition to this, co-innovation also drives co-ideation and co-institutionalization drives co-innovation. On top of this, several innovation cycles can occur at the same time and affect one another.

Figure 1.1 visualizes the model of linear, cyclic and interactive eco- and sustainable innovation through co-ideation, co-innovation and co-institutionalization. The three managerial levels in the system are symbolized by the dotted circles. The dotted circle in the center represents the co-ideation level. The surrounding dotted circle visualizes the co-innovation level. The outer dotted circle represents the co-institutionalization level. The double-headed arrows between the dotted circles visualize the linear, circular and interactive influence between these levels. The balls in the figure, situated on the dotted circles, visualize the elements at each level. The co-ideation level consists of leaders, champions and entrepreneurs; the co-innovation level consists of teams, projects, businesses and public-private partnerships; and the co-institutionalization level consists of market and society, knowledge and technology, and policy and regulation. This section briefly introduces these elements. The next chapters in this book are successively dedicated to one of these ten elements and delve into more details. The book concludes with a chapter that interprets the model as a whole.

Co-ideation

Three distinctive individual roles or personal behaviors play a pivotal role in the co-ideation process: the leader or leadership, the entrepreneur or entrepreneurship, and the champion or championship. The leaders, entrepreneurs and champions can be seen as the main drivers of the ideation process, that is, the development of ideas to innovate in sustainability. They also drive the co-ideation process by cooperating with one another and with other members of their organizations in order to share and further develop their thoughts and plans.

Leaders

Individual leadership directs a sustainable innovation team toward new creative ideas. To direct a creative process, the leader can choose from a repertoire of leadership styles and skills. A leader who wants to adopt a charismatic style, for example, can choose to energize colleagues to innovate and to have an accelerating effect on people's innovative activity (Murphy and Ensher, 2008; Paulsen, Maldonado, Callan and Ayoko, 2009). A leader can also be more oriented toward formal management instruments and put an emphasis on a strict structuring and control of sustainable innovation activities of workers in the firm (Abernethy, Bouwens and Van Lent, 2010). In addition, a leader who wants to act more strategically can use his or her hierarchical power base to motivate, force or direct teams to innovate in sustainability (Carmeli, Gelbard and Gefen, 2010). A leader can also choose to have frequent contact and cooperation with coworkers. A leader who likes to interact with colleagues can choose to empower others to innovate and to enable them to become sustainable innovation leaders themselves and help the official leader (Crevani, Lindgren and Packendorff, 2010).

Entrepreneurs

Not just leadership alone fuels the ideation process. It is also the entrepreneur or individual with entrepreneurial spirit who contributes to ideation and co-ideation. The entrepreneur can be seen as a main force behind the ideation strategies and processes in organizations. The entrepreneur, for example, can take the initiative to develop new products and services and can be the one who is constantly looking for new ways to make money. It is often mentioned that he or she always sees where new opportunities to sell products arise, "smells" where the opportunities for new services are hidden and starts projects and ventures to launch products and services and to open markets (Beveridge and Guy, 2005). It can be said that the entrepreneurial person is driven by the possibilities of successful innovation and is not scared by the risks of failure (Dixon and Clifford, 2007; Klein Woolthuis, 2009). In today's business landscape, socially driven entrepreneurship seems to be becoming a powerful alternative to gain strategic advantage, to mobilize resources, to raise the profile of the organizations involved and to generate income in new and emerging markets (Di Domenico and Haugh, 2007).

Champions

A third important driver of the ideation and co-ideation process is the innovation champion. Innovation champions are often seen as the creative drivers of innovative ideas and initiatives. An innovation champion, for example, endorses innovation by persuading others to join a project or, by means of a lobby, getting top management on board for an innovative venture. The champion of innovation talks innovation all the time (Kelley and Lee, 2010), has the expertise to innovate and likes to generate ideas (Sim, Griffin, Price and Vojak, 2007). The innovation champion processes information that generates new ideas, traces and shares knowledge and looks for the trends from which to derive new ideas (Coakes and Smith, 2007).

In the literature, these three types of individuals are judged to be the main drivers behind the ideation process of sustainable innovation. Cooperation among these three types and cooperation with other colleagues in the organization can contribute to the co-ideation process in the firm.

Co-innovation

Four organizational forms play a crucial role in the co-innovation process: the team, the project, the business and the public-private partnership. The work in and cooperation between individuals in teams, projects, businesses and public-private partnerships transform the ideas that originate at the co-ideation level into new sustainable and profitable business proposals. They also bring the ideas to the next level: the co-innovation level, where the ideas can be realized.

Teams

The leaders, entrepreneurs and champions of eco- and sustainable innovation need to cooperate with others in organizational settings. They need an organizational context; otherwise, their activities remain unnoticed. They, for example, need a team of generalists and specialists to adopt their ideas and develop these into new processes, products and services that actually change and rejuvenate business. An idea that is promoted by a leader, an entrepreneurial person or an innovation champion often has to be developed into something that can be made by the firm. This implies that a team of colleagues can be assigned by a company to structurally and coherently work on interesting ideas (Björkman, 2004; Hülsheger, Anderson and Salgado, 2009). They can be asked to separate the creative ideas with market potential from the ideas that will probably fail (Kratzer, Leenders and Van Engelen, 2006; Mathisen and Torsheim, 2006). Research indicates that an innovative team needs to be guided by a culture or spirit that supports the search for and discovery of practical ways to turn ideas into something that can be made by the firm (Adarves-Yorno, Postmes and Haslam, 2007; Martinsuo, 2009).

Projects

Often, projects are used as a main organizational form to structure a company's first attempt to develop a new innovative practice. A varied set of management principles can be applied to coordinate and control sustainably innovative activities in innovation projects. A project, for example, can start with a well-prepared project plan and use this as the basic outline for planning actions, deadlines and deliverables (Dorenbosch, Van Engen and Verhagen, 2005; Dougherty, 2008). In addition to this, a project organization can also choose to plan the innovations step by step and to commit all participants to a collective schedule. The project can focus on agreements and on monitoring progress from start to finish (Keegan and Turner, 2002; Killen, Hunt and Kleinschmidt, 2008). Furthermore, the project organization can develop a strategic view of what kind of newness it has to deliver to the world outside (Newell, Goussevskaia, Swan, Bresnen and Obembe, 2008). It can define and realize innovation goals that fit with the strategy of the firm (Kenney, 2003; Plambeck and Taylor, 2007). The innovation project is often used to develop innovations with which firms can (re)gain a competitive advantage in the marketplace. For this, it is important that the project members listen to customer demand and use both customer and user information to translate ideas into processes, products and services with market potential (Beverland, 2005).

Businesses

The innovation teams and projects are mainly situated in firms. In addition, firms often run more projects at the same time and have portfolios of various co-innovative projects. In modern business, it is common practice for team members to participate in several projects at the same time, for projects to be linked and for projects to evolve into other projects. In many cases, different firms cooperate in innovation projects, for example to share complementary knowledge, to serve larger markets or to gain power in the competitive field. Cooperative innovation among several firms, teams and projects is a complex organizational challenge. Co-innovating firms try to choose a new innovative direction and usually start to explore the possibilities for going it alone. When that is not possible, companies that do not want to give up explore the opportunities to co-innovate with others (Dell'Era and Verganti, 2009; Spithoven, Claryse and Knockaert, 2010).

They then have to negotiate about the resources each organization has to bring in and about the revenues each will get in return when the innovations become a commercial success (Nieto and Santamaría, 2007; Vuola and Hameri, 2006). To organize the co-innovative process, they have to develop innovation plans with one another and establish joint ventures in which these innovations are cooperatively developed, built (Rampersad, Quester and Troshani, 2010; Vuola and Hameri, 2006) and sold (Calia, Guerrini and Moura, 2007; Van de Vrande, De Jong, Vanhaverbeke and De Rochemont, 2009).

Public-Private Partnerships

Co-innovating firms often choose to experiment in a public-private partnership before they really decide to enter the market with new processes, products and services (Harborne and Hendry, 2009; Hendry, Harborne and Brown, 2010). In a pilot, demonstration or joint public-private experiment, innovative sustainable options can be tested, developed and prepared for use in regular business. Public-private partnerships enable governmental and commercial organizations to experiment and gain experience with sustainable issues, technologies and co-innovative procedures and routines (Foxon, Gross, Chase, Howes, Arnall and Anderson, 2005). Often the government subsidizes an eco-innovative demonstration project and wants to cooperate with commercial firms and help them to develop sustainable business. In return, the government wants companies to invest equally in the project, for example by means of investments in terms of man-hours, the input of advanced knowledge and the inclusion of top managers. Public and private actors who want to sustain a longer-term relationship build public-private partnerships with clear and longer-term visions on sustainability, often have some experience and knowledge with eco- and sustainable innovation and share the same ambitions, for example a desire to create an important new sustainable product or production process (Garvin and Bosso, 2008). Public-private partnerships can last for many years and have a remarkable influence on the innovativeness of industry. Organizations that participate in public-private partnerships develop new areas of competence in the field of sustainability that can give them a competitive advantage in a sustainable market of the future.

These four organizational forms are the main drivers of the innovation process for sustainability. Cooperative linkages and ties among teams, projects, businesses and public-private partnerships contribute to the co-innovation processes in and among organizations in industry.

Co-institutionalization

Three business environmental forces play an important role at the co-institutionalization level: market and society, knowledge and technology, and policy and regulation. Interaction among these business environmental forces constitutes the co-institutional environment that enables commercial firms to grow their emerging sustainable businesses into mature ones with a large impact on industry and society.

Market and Society

The business environment exercises considerable influence on organizations' sustainable activities. It is often stated that firms innovate because the market wants them to. In the past, firms' strategies changed over the years because markets continuously exerted pressure on companies to innovate. Due to the emergence of new sustainability-aware customer groups that ask for eco-innovative and sustainable products and services, firms may start to realize that sustainability may have a lot of market potential. In business, some highly innovative companies start to invest in eco- and sustainable innovation and aim to open these emerging markets (Ozaki and Sevastyanova, 2011). In the meantime, governmental and commercial organizations have to deal with increasing pressure from society to contribute to the solution of ecological, social and societal problems. Dominant environmental sustainability issues that, for example, dominate societal discussions and put pressure on companies to improve performance are pollution and emission control, protection of welfare and human rights, and a desire for a better world for present and future generations (Brundtland and Khalid, 1987; Esty, Levy, Srebotnjak and De Sherbinin, 2005).

Knowledge and Technology

Continuous technological progress enables firms to innovate and pushes customers to buy technological innovations. A technological capability that stimulates companies' innovativeness is their capability to combine and recombine their existing knowledge repertoire with newly developed and appropriated knowledge. Companies with a (re)combination strategy know how to constantly introduce new and improved versions of their products and services. They constantly refresh and renew their product and service lines with the newest sustainable gadgets, features and more fundamental changes in sustainability. Technological progress enables them to be leading innovators in their field of business. A company's capability to be on the front line and set trends can motivate customers to follow and adopt the new products and services. Firms with a technology leadership strategy are often seen as major change agents in industry (Kunz and Warren, 2011).

Policy and Regulation

Another key element at the co-institutionalization level is policy and regulation. Depending on the political climate, the government plans and executes environmental and sustainable policy and subsidizes, funds and regulates sustainably innovative initiatives and programs in the country. Governmental action can have considerable influence on industry. Research indicates that when the government funds an innovation project and demands a high level of innovation in return, this indeed has a significant positive effect on the project's innovativeness (Bjørnåli and Gulbrandsen, 2010). National regulation can be a powerful institutional tool. It can stimulate innovators and discourage laggards from going on with unsustainable practices. Sometimes strict regulation can be necessary, for example, when emissions need to be reduced. In other cases, performance-based regulation, that is, regulation that stimulates organizations to innovate in a certain direction without strictly defined norms and measures, appears to be more effective and challenges firms to develop their own innovative solutions and approaches (Wagner and Llerena, 2011).

These three business environmental forces can have a major influence on the eco-innovative and sustainable climate in industry and define the institutional conditions for eco-innovative and sustainable co-ideation and co-innovation. Interaction between private firms and public organizations shapes the industrial environment in which new co-innovative sustainable practices can become institutionalized. It sets boundaries for deviating practices and enables sustainable business to grow.

1.3   RESEARCH METHODOLOGY

The eco-innovation and sustainability model is based on extensive literature research and on widespread empirical research in Dutch industry. The research approach of Van Aken (2005) is used as the basic methodology to develop the model. One of the basic principles of Van Aken's (2005) research methodology is that theoretical and empirical research can be conducted to construct a model, heuristic or theory that serves as a guideline or frame of reference for managers and that enables them to act and to manage a practical setting. The aim of this book thus is to design a theory-based and empirically grounded model of the process of eco-innovation and sustainability in industry. The book aims to provide insights for practitioners into how eco- and sustainable innovation can be controlled and managed. To researchers, the model aims to enable and guide further research into the workings of eco-innovation and sustainability systems. In line with this, the research in this book consists of three interrelated steps, that is: (1) shaping the research model, (2) conducting additional theoretical and empirical studies, and (3) analyzing and synthesizing the studies' outcomes into a coherent model.

Step 1.   Shaping the Research Model

The research model is based on twenty years of theoretical and empirical research into eco-innovation management processes in the Dutch house building industry (Bossink, 2002a, b, c; 2004a, b; 2007a, b; 2008; 2009a, b; 2011a, b; Bossink and Brouwers, 1996). Previous publications in this research trajectory analyze and discuss the function of leaders (Bossink, 2004a; 2007a; 2011a), entrepreneurs (Bossink, 2011a, b), champions (Bossink, 2004a; 2007a; 2011a), teams (Bossink, 2002b; 2011a), projects (Bossink, 2002b; 2011a; Bossink and Brouwers, 1996), businesses (Bossink, 2002c; 2011a), public-private partnerships (Bossink, 2002a; 2007b; 2008; 2009a, b; 2011a), market and society (Bossink, 2004b; 2011a), knowledge and technology (Bossink, 2004b; 2011a) and policy and regulation (Bossink, 2002a; 2004b; 2011a) in the eco- and sustainable innovation system of Dutch house building. A synthesis of the elements into a coherent model that describes the eco- and sustainable innovation system is published in Bossink (2011a) (for a summary of some of the main conclusions of this study see Appendix 1). The model claims analytical value for research and practice in similar settings, that is, the building industries and project-based industries. However, the question remains whether and to what degree the model can claim analytical validity for industrial settings other than the building industries and project-based industries. This question is the point of departure of the research in this book (Van Aken, 2005). The book builds on the results from the previous studies of Bossink, conducts additional theoretical research in (eco and sustainable) innovation management literature and carries out new exploratory empirical research in several other sectors of Dutch industry. It aims to de-sign a model with increased analytical validity for industry in general.

Step 2.   Conducting Additional Theoretical and Empirical Studies

Additional theoretical studies are conducted with respect to all elements of the model (co-ideation: leaders, entrepreneurs and champions; co-innovation: teams, projects, businesses and public-private partnerships; co-institutionalization: markets and society, knowledge and technology, and policy and regulation). Literature databases are consulted for publications on ecological, green, social, societal and sustainable innovation in business and industry and for each element of the model. In addition to this, for all elements of the model, except for the champions element, additional empirical studies are conducted, mainly by interviewing managers and experts in various industries in the Netherlands. Table 1.1 gives an overview of the new empirical material that is used in this book.

All empirical research is conducted by master's-degree students and supervised by the author of this book. The interviews are taken, recorded and analyzed by students in the master's-degree program in business administration at VU University Amsterdam. The interviews are based on open questions related to the main elements of the model of eco-innovation and sustainability. The interviewees are given maximum freedom to elaborate on issues that relate to the elements of the model. This facilitated in-depth conversations between researcher and interviewee. The interviews are recorded, transcribed and either manually coded and analyzed or coded and analyzed with the help of computer software (Atlas.ti; MAXQDA; NVivo).

Table 1.1   Overview of Empirical Studies in this Book

# Expert interviews	Industry	Reported by	Interviews interpreted and quoted in chapter
6	Horticulture	Brockhoff (2011)	2
10	Various industries	Klawer (2008)	3
6	Building	Bossink (2011a)	4
10	Metal	Van der Wiel (2010)	5
13	Banking	Verloop (2008)	6
10	Various industries	Mahawat Khan (2010)	7
10	Food	De Bruijn (2009)	8
30	Various industries	Indriani (2009)	9
9	Food	De Swaaf (2008)	10
10	Trade	Roeloffzen (2010)	11

The original reports can be obtained from the website http://www.ub.vu.nl. Empirical interpretations and quotations in this book are respectively based on and taken from these reports. For readability, some quotations have been edited, but the original scope and content remain intact.

Step 3.   Analyzing and Synthesizing the Studies' Outcomes

As a result of the additional theoretical and empirical studies all elements of Bossink's (2011a) model are articulated, adjusted, complemented or changed, resulting in an model of eco-innovation and sustainability with increased analytical value for industry (see Figure 1.1).

1.4   COMPARISON WITH OTHER APPROACHES

To put the model of eco-innovation and sustainability management into a broader theoretical perspective this section compares the model with two other streams in the literature. The model will be compared with the national environmental planning approach and the national systems of innovation stream. This comparison results in an overview of similarities and differences. The section starts with a description of the basic aspects of the two alternative theoretical approaches and continues with the comparison.

National Environmental Policy Planning

The first approach to be summarized here is the national environmental policy planning approach. In 2006, Kivimaa and Mickwitz introduced a coherent model of systemic eco-innovation. It is derived from Finnish practice and claims analytical validity for other industrial countries. According to Kivimaa and Mickwitz (2006), sustainable innovation starts with the development of a general sustainable innovation plan for the country as a whole, and this is made by officials from the authorities, universities and larger firms. Once the plan is completed, the nation's governmental and commercial organizations can take the next step. They derive action plans from the basic plans and can try to execute these. Kivimaa and Mickwitz (2006) describe and visualize environmental policy planning as a top-down process. The basic sustainability plan is made on a central national level, and then all cooperating organizations are supposed to work according to the guidelines of this plan. Kivimaa and Mickwitz (2006) propose that this top-down system of environmental policy planning consists of three basic levels: policy strategies, policy instruments and policy outcomes. The first basic level thus is policy strategies. On this level, the government takes responsibility and leads the process. Representatives of the government, national institutions, research centers and commercial organizations strategically review environmental policies of the past. They use the insights that result from these reviews to develop a new environmental strategy for the nation. The environmental policy strategy initiates and influences a second level of the national system, which is labeled policy instruments. At this level, representatives from governmental, institutional, scientific and commercial organizations define several large national strategic environmental programs. The environmental programs consist of broad portfolios of environmental technology and projects and comprise a coherent set of assigned environmental objectives and allocated financial and human resources. The programs initiate the third level of the system, which is called policy outcomes. On this level, both fundamental and more applied research and development (R&D) projects are planned and executed. Governmental, institutional, scientific and commercial organizations cooperatively develop new innovative environmental technologies and practices. These eco-technologies and -practices then have to diffuse to other firms in the nation's industry. The impact of this top-down system of national environmental policy planning can be measured periodically and becomes the starting point for a new nationwide and top-down process of environmental policy planning.

National Systems of Innovation

The second approach to be described here is the national systems of innovation approach. To a certain degree, the national systems of innovation approach is comparable with Kivimaa and Mickwitz's (2006) model of national environmental planning. Both build on the same types of actors, and both propose that cooperation among these actors directly stimulates innovation on a national level. According to Bartholomew (1997), one of the proponents of the national systems of innovation approach, the four basic actor types of a national innovation system are the government, research institutions, educational institutions and industry. Lundvall, Johnson, Andersen and Dalum (2002) draw a similar picture. According to them, a national system of innovation consists of institutions, users and producers.

Bartholomew (1997) contends that research organizations and industrial firms form the center of the nation's innovation system, and government and educational organizations can be seen as satellites that can strengthen the research organizations' and industrial firms' function. The national innovation system concentrates primarily on the development of knowledge and the application of this knowledge in industry. Lundvall, Johnson, Andersen and Dalum (2002) present a similar point of view. They contend that the coordination, cooperation and interactive learning process among agents of the institutions, users and producers forms a strong dynamic driver of national innovativeness. According to Bartholomew (1997), the centers of the system are innovative because of the knowledge they possess and exploit. The development of knowledge in the industrial firms, the first center of the innovation system, is stimulated by the accumulation of technological knowledge in industrial sectors that are related and also by cooperation with other organizations in R&D and innovation projects. The development of a body of knowledge in the nation's research organizations, which is the second center of the innovation system, is supported by the research centers' international contacts and working relationships with foreign counterparts, the nation's tradition of funding of basic research and the national practice of scientific education. Bartholomew (1997) also mentions several other factors that stimulate the flow of knowledge between the two centers of the countrywide improvement scheme: the commercial orientation of research institutions and their collaboration with industrial firms, the mobility of labor in the country, the willingness of venture capitalists to invest in innovative public-private partnerships and a government that actively invests in a knowledge economy.

Eco-innovation and Sustainability Management in Perspective

Table 1.2 gives a concise overview of differences and similarities between the model of eco-innovation and sustainability management in this book and the two alternative approaches in the literature.

The first row of Table 1.2 shows differences among all three approaches. The innovation mechanism that forms the heart of the eco-innovation and sustainability model in this book is of a managerial nature. It supposes that eco-innovation and sustainability are something that can be planned, controlled, organized and coordinated and that they can be shaped, controlled and developed by key individuals such as entrepreneurs and project managers in commercial firms. This differs from the national environmental policy approach, which builds on the assumption that environmental innovation is a top-down policy planning process that is induced by the government. It also differs from the national systems of innovation approach, which supposes

Table 1.2   Eco-innovation and Sustainability Management in Perspective

	Eco-innovation and sustainability management	National environmental policy planning	National innovation systems
Innovation mechanism	Management process induced by key individuals in firms	Top-down policy planning process induced by the government	Knowledge flow and learning processes among universities and firms
Innovation dynamic	Cooperation and interaction	Logical structure of strategies, programs and actions	Cooperation and interaction
Innovating entity	Professionals and firms	Policymakers	Knowledge workers
Innovation scope	Eco-innovation and sustainability	Eco-innovation	Innovation in the broadest sense

that knowledge flow and learning processes among authorities, universities and firms are key innovation mechanisms.

The second row of Table 1.2 shows a similarity between the model in this book and the national systems of innovation approach and a difference between the model in this book and the national environmental planning approach. A basic assumption of the model of eco-innovation and sustainability in this book is that the innovation process is linear, cyclic and interactive at the same time. The main innovation dynamic is cooperation and interaction among actors, the organizations they represent and the institutional structures wherein these organizations are situated. This differs from the national environmental policy planning approach. The main innovation dynamic behind the national environmental policy planning approach is that eco-innovation starts with a national policy, which is transformed into action plans and projects in practice. It assumes that the actions are logically derived from plans and that these plans stem logically from policies, strategies and vision statements. Last, this book's eco-innovation and sustainability model and the national innovation systems approach have in common that both build on cooperation and interaction among actors as the main dynamic that drives the innovation process.

The third row of Table 1.2 shows that all models mention different entities as drivers of innovation in the system. The eco-innovation and sustainability model in this book assumes that innovation thrives on the enthusiasm, drive, confidence, vision and hands-on mentality of professionals in organizations. The national environmental policy planning approach draws a somewhat different picture. The central innovation-driving actor there is the policymaker who writes vision documents that are translated by other officials into actionable programs and that are developed into practical projects by hands-on practitioners. Finally, the national systems of innovation approach models innovation as a process that is stimulated by knowledge workers in universities, laboratories and firms that interactively develop, share and apply new knowledge and thereby innovate.

Finally, the fourth row in Table 1.2 shows that the type of innovation the model concentrates on is different for all three models. The eco-innovation and sustainability management model in this book addresses eco-innovation and sustainability, which comprise environmental innovations, social innovations and societal innovations. It covers sustainable innovation in the broadest sense of the word or concept. The national environmental planning approach works with a more narrow scope and concentrates on environmental and ecological innovations. Finally, the national systems of innovation approach has the broadest view of all three and concentrates on innovation in general. It deals with all kinds of innovations and does not specify the type of innovation.

1.5   SUMMARY

Eco- and sustainable innovation needs to be managed at three cooperative levels. At the first, so-called co-ideation level, leaders, entrepreneurs and champions cooperatively develop the important new sustainably innovative ideas. At the second level, the co-innovative level, they cooperate and interact with one another and with other coworkers and professionals in organizational settings such as teams, projects, businesses and public-private partnerships to actually transform these ideas into business. At the third level, the co-institutionalization level, professionals from commercial, governmental and not-for-profit and nongovernmental organizations cooperate and interact to build institutional structures and arrangements that enable sustainable business to grow large. This approach proposes that eco-innovation and sustainability originate from key individuals in organizations, are realized by organizations and are institutionalized by efforts to create an infrastructure that enables organizations to grow into major players in industry. Activities at all three levels of the innovation system contribute to the process of eco- and sustainable innovation.

This book consists of twelve chapters, of which this first chapter introduced the basic model. The next ten chapters consecutively present the elements of the co-ideation, co-innovation and co-institutionalization levels of the model. The twelfth and final chapter concludes with a discussion of the model as a whole. The next chapter delves into the first element at the co-ideation level of the model, which is leaders and leadership.

2 Co-ideation by Leaders

2.1 INTRODUCTION

The first category of key players at the co-ideation level is the category of leaders. Eco-innovative and sustainable leadership is more than leadership in the traditional sense of the word. It builds on traditional leadership aspects but adds new characteristics to it. The eco-innovative and sustainable leader has many responsibilities and needs various skills to perform right. Such a leader has a time-consuming job and has to be multiskilled. The eco-innovative and sustainable leader needs a certain degree of charisma and has to communicate with a vision that helps subordinates to contribute to the innovative ambitions of the firm. An eco-innovative and sustainable leader also must be experienced with management instruments that facilitate planning and development of innovative activity in the company. A competent leader needs a well-formed strategic vision of what the firm could achieve in the near future. Moreover, the leader has to be people oriented and a human among humans. The leader has to cooperate with others, empower coworkers to contribute to the firm and communicate with various stakeholder groups the company wants to serve. On top of this, the sustainable leader also has to know and feel what the company's enduring purpose and value are for society and has to act on a wider time frame than tomorrow or the next year. A sustainable leader has a feel for what is needed to increase a firm's trustworthiness in business and society. The sustainable leader has access to this broad array of skills and behaviors. Leadership is the first element at the co-ideation level of the model of eco-innovation and sustainability management (see Figure 2.1).

This chapter first describes theory that forms the basis of the sustainable leadership element of the model (Section 2.2). It introduces the research methods that are used to increase the analytical validity of the model for industry (Section 2.3). It then explores the analytical value of the leadership element of the model in practice (Section 2.4) and in theory (Section 2.5). The chapter concludes with a summary of the main characteristics of the leadership element at the co-ideation level (Section 2.6).

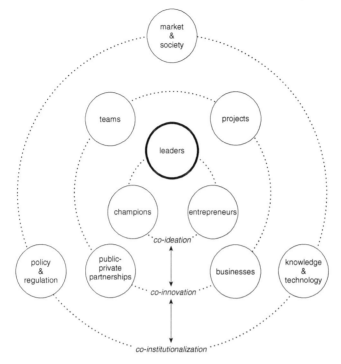

Figure 2.1   Co-ideation by leaders.

2.2   THEORETICAL BASIS

The leadership function has many characteristics and comprises many behaviors that are difficult for one person to perform. In addition to that, the leader who wants to guide a firm toward eco-innovation and sustainability has to give something extra. A modern leader has vision, knows how to control a company, is an experienced strategist and is good with people. A sustainable leader needs all these skills but must also be capable of monitoring and improving the societal position of the company and embed it as a responsible entity in industry and society.

Charisma

Charismatic leadership deals with generating energy, with creating commitment and directing coworkers toward new objectives, values or aspirations. To put it simply: it catalyzes innovation (Paulsen, Maldonado, Callan and Ayoko, 2009). Jung, Wu and Chow (2008) argue that the charismatic leader has a strong vision and neglects organizational boundaries to communicate this to coworkers to and stimulate them to contribute to renewal.

Mumford and Licuanan (2004) establish that a charismatic leader develops visions of the future that are attractive and that attract followers. Such visions consider the underlying needs and values of key stakeholders of the organization. They are intellectually stimulating and ask people to think of the company's societal function. According to Murphy and Ensher (2008), charismatic leaders are powerful managers of highly creative teams. Charismatic leaders tell members of the company what the idealized goal of the future is, and they spend considerable time and energy building social cohesion and mutual respect in teams. They want to surprise people with unconventional actions and ideas with which they hope people will engage.

Control

A leader also has to behave in a managerial way and be a manager who manages. The controlling manager sets goals people have to accomplish, establishes standards that have to be met and defines roles and responsibilities for team members to do a proper job. The managing leader creates organizational systems and processes to measure, monitor and assess results and corrective action and, through these, tries to get the company under control. Controlling management relies upon management instruments that focus on the facts of the company. Examples of control-enabling management instruments are a computer-aided system for project planning and a meeting structure that facilitates the review of the results of cooperation between departments in the organization (Burton and Obel, 1998). In line with Burton and Obel (1998), Abernethy, Bouwens and Van Lent (2010) argue that a controlling leadership style influences the use of planning and control systems. They document how managerial leaders use a formal system of planning and control to communicate goals, deadlines, targets and measures to their agents in the firm. The leader uses these instruments to control subordinates and at the same time to provide them clear measures that empowers them to take responsibility.

Strategy

Managers performing a strategic innovation leadership style know the strategic competences of their organization and align their personal strategies with the firm's strategy. Halbesleben, Novicevic, Harvey and Buckley (2003) argue that a strategic innovation leader facilitates the development of the innovative capabilities of employees. People get time and resources to work on personal development and improve their performance. Strategic leaders are committed to innovation and invest in it. They know that investments in people are necessary. Carmeli, Gelbard and Gefen (2010) define the strategic leadership style as leadership that cultivates "a balance between bureaucracy and anarchy, as well as influencing the structure of interconnections of organizational systems, constructs a system with creative and innovative responsiveness which is a key to enabling change and adaptation"

(p. 341). According to Carmeli, Gelbard and Gefen (2010) strategic leadership contributes to the "strategic fit" of the firm and, by this, to the firm's performance in the long run. With respect to this, the concept of "strategic fit" is defined as the degree to which the firm is able to sustain a competitive position on the marketplace. The strategic leader invests in people and in firm viability.

Interaction

Crevani, Lindgren and Packendorff (2010) propose that leadership is a practice that is exercised in human interactions between leaders and subordinates. They contend that leadership processes are "continuous processes where performative norms meet the specifics of everyday muddling-through, where people both enable and circumscribe themselves and others, where perceptions of emerging structure and emerging ambiguity are constantly handled in interaction" (p. 84). An interactive innovation leadership style concentrates on individualized consideration when providing support, coaching and guidance to people. Because of this leadership style, when there is frequent and intense contact between leader and follower, followers sometimes develop into complementary leaders and take responsibility for aspects of the leader's leadership tasks (Fleming and Waguespack, 2007).

Societal Impact

The literature review illustrates that modern leadership puts quite a burden on the shoulders of the persons who lead. In addition, the sustainable leader has to be capable of more than this. The sustainable leader also has to ensure that the firm has a caring, responsible and sensible impact on society. It is often pointed out that native Indians still have a direct relationship with the earth. They call it "Mother Earth" and feel themselves embraced and nurtured by it. It is often written and said that Indians really understand that nature gives to humans and therefore should be served by humans. The natural cycles of the earth support people, and people are part of these cycles, not masters of the universe. It is often stated that modern people have lost this sense of reality. A stream in the literature concentrates on a more nature-oriented approach to leadership; recently, concepts like "agrarian leadership" and "honeybee leadership" have emerged in the academic discourse. Green and McCann (2011), for example, coined the concept of agrarian leadership and argue that there is a real need for better management of natural resources. According to Green and McCann (2011), agrarians and their desires, methods and technologies provide better support to the environment than our current modern industrial business practices. Green and McCann (2011) argue that human values that form the basis of agrarian leadership, including independence, hard work, family focus, trustworthiness and an organic view, are important values for sustainable leadership of the future. Agrarian leadership means that the leader adopts a long-term timeframe, which is at least generational. This differs completely from a one- to five-year strategic planning horizon or a stakeholder-first model, approaches that many firms are used to. The agrarian leader understands that delivering maximum value to shareholders for five consecutive years can also mean that the "soil for business" impoverishes the land and that yields can stagnate. The agrarian leader understands that a more balanced approach can generate revenues that can be sustained. Adopting an agrarian view on the position of the firm in industry and in society is maybe both a more ethical way of doing business as well as a more profitable way. In line with this, Surie and Ashley (2008) argue that the integration of ethical thinking and acting into the leadership function is a condition for firms that want to create sustainable value for the longer term. They contend that successful leaders of corporate social responsibility programs recognize that being ethical can contribute to the brand value of the company and to its trustworthiness and legitimacy (for more information of corporate social responsibility, see Appendix 7). Development and introduction of new sustainable products and services can be very important because "leaders who start new ventures or change the existing organization through the development of a new product or innovation are catalysts for change and engaged in the process of creating a new reality" (p. 239). To broaden the repertoire of the responsible leader, Avery and Bergsteiner (2011a) introduce the role of the so-called honeybee leader. This means that the leader "builds communities, fosters collaboration among stakeholders and promotes long-term value" (p. 11). This is in contrast with the "locust leader," which refers to "images of swarms of voracious insects descending on green fields and stripping them bare" (p. 11). According to Avery and Bergsteiner (2011b), firms need to adopt a culture that is based on teamwork instead of on personal scores and individual bonuses. Collaboration needs to exceed the specific project or department and even the boundaries of the firm. Collaboration with suppliers and even competitors may also be considered. Cooperation at all these levels can result in co-development of new products and services that make a difference and contribute to a sustainable future.

2.3   RESEARCH METHOD

Additional empirical and theoretical studies are performed to further increase the generic value of the leadership element of the model of eco-innovation and sustainability management for industry.

Step 1.   Shaping the Research Model

This chapter builds on the results from the initial study of Bossink (2011a) (see Appendix 1) and focuses on the leadership element of the model (Section 2.2). It conducts exploratory empirical research in the Dutch horticulture industry to investigate how the leadership element of the model holds for another empirical context (Section 2.4) and conducts further theoretical research in eco-innovation management to explore whether this element can be shaped toward a broader generic analytical for industry (Section 2.5).

Step 2.   Conducting Theoretical and Empirical Studies

Literature databases are consulted for research papers on leadership for ecological, green, social, societal and sustainable innovation in business, firms and industry. In addition to this, six managers in the Dutch horticulture industry are interviewed and asked to reflect on the sustainability issues they think are important in their work, company and industry (Brockhoff, 2011).

Step 3.   Analyzing and Synthesizing the Studies' Outcomes

The leadership element in the initial model (Bossink, 2011a) is confronted with the additional theoretical and empirical studies. On the basis of the outcomes of this analysis, the characteristics of the leadership element at the co-ideation level of the model are defined for industry (Section 2.5).

2.4   EXPLORING THE EMPIRICAL FIELD

The respondents agree that various forms of leadership can have a stimulating impact on eco-innovation and sustainability in business. The exploratory interviews indicate that charisma, control, strategy, interaction and societal impact can be the main elements of an eco-innovative and sustainable leadership function in a firm. This section is the author's interpretation of Brockhoff (2011), and quotations are taken from that source.

Charisma

All respondents explain that top managers and other leading persons in the firm are perceived by others to be role models. Being a role model is considered an important social instrument in motivating other people to act in more eco-aware and sustainable ways. One of the interviewees, for example, illustrates the effect of a role model as follows: "We tell our directors that they need to be aware of the fact that they are figureheads. People look at them! And much more than directors think!" (p. 47). All respondents stress that it is important that a leader inspires people to become eco-innovative thinkers and actors themselves. A respondent elaborates on this by saying that to be able to inspire others, the leader must really believe in corporate sustainability. People do not follow an insecure leader but need vision and direction. A respondent puts it this way: "The leader needs the capability to tell the story right"; this is important "in making [subordinates] enthusiastic and inspired" (p. 48). Another interviewee states in this respect that to enhance team spirit, an eco-innovation leader should "take the team by the hand. You will notice that [the team members] will start generating ideas themselves" (p. 48).

Control

Most respondents elaborate on the necessity of a corporate coordination plan to set and manage eco-innovative goals and objectives. The goals that can be derived from such a plan can be integrated into the policy of the organization and should be monitored periodically. With respect to monitoring, the interviewees agree that people have to be made responsible and accountable for sustainable activity. An interviewee argues that the people responsible are also the ones to be praised or criticized. "It is important to criticize division managers and directors to the extent they are actively involved in achieving the goals we set. The goals need to be formulated in such a way that the manager becomes involved. . . . A Manager needs to show what (s)he did, how (s)he invested in his/her employees, the environment and the value chain" (p. 57). Respondents agree that eco-innovative goals need to be concrete and have to be quantifiable. In particular, long-term goals such as energy and water reduction need to be monitored. One of the interviewees explains this as follows: "On a monthly basis, we control the total usage of energy and water. In case the results are disappointing we will discuss this with the responsible person to verify the reasons, and to define what needs to be done" (p. 57).

Strategy

Almost all respondents are convinced that eco-innovation and sustainability are of strategic importance to the firm. An interviewee, for example, states that corporate sustainability is part of his firm's strategy and receives considerable attention. He remarks that sustainability has to be adopted by the whole firm: "Sustainability requires critical analysis and questioning of all elements of the organization. You have to know where to improve. Corporate social responsibility is not a trend. It must be integrated in your strategy, by means of plans" (p. 40). Another interviewee is convinced that when sustainability is integrated into the strategy of the organization, the organization creates opportunities for a new kind of business: "Sustainability is not a fashion word we can just use by coincidence. It is not a 'tool.' . . . Sustainability must be related to a palette of who you are, what you do, and for whom you do it. This is a difficult task for leaders" (p. 39). Such a new kind of business may be a profitable business, as long as it concentrates on a sound business model. One of the interviewees remarks that it is important that managers communicate and explain the firm's sustainability strategy to their employees and encourage people to join the firm's sustainability approach: "Employees also have to figure out things themselves. . . . It is important to acknowledge that ideas are also generated bottom-up" (p. 49). It means that top-down sustainable strategy can feed and be fed by bottom-up ideas and commitment.

Interaction

The respondents agree that eco-innovation and sustainability are often not sufficiently visualized and communicated to the employees of the firm. They think that more efforts can be put into communication, for example, by publishing articles in the company newspaper, on the corporate website, and in communication campaigns that focus on corporate sustainability. In this respect, an interviewee argues that employees have to be informed about the results of sustainable projects and about the environmental effects of their firm's practices. It is important that employees become committed to and responsible for this relatively new issue. All interviewees confirm that involving people from the start contributes to development of new ideas. An interviewee is very explicit about this. To him, people's involvement and commitment are a prerequisite to really energizing the innovative process. He states that people should be invited periodically by management to exchange knowledge about strategic issues and thus also about sustainability and eco-affairs. He has done this himself, and one result of this practice has been that the logistics of his firm have improved in effectiveness and efficiency and also reduced CO_2 emissions.

Societal Impact

Most respondents are convinced that ethical issues have to be addressed. Social issues such as working conditions and environmental considerations such as reductions in waste, energy use and water pollution have to be dealt with by companies. A respondent states, for example: "The core message is: Sustainability Everywhere! Consider carefully your position in this world" (p. 39). The respondents agree that it is necessary that their organizations take responsibility for sustainable business. An interviewee, for example, states that "we need . . . a code of conduct. It is a challenging task for leaders to manage this" (p. 41). All respondents consider eco-innovativeness and sustainability to be their company's obligation as a market leader and important player in business. They agree that their firm has to set new standards to show what matters and has to be the first to take responsibility. In addition to this, they think that doing so strengthens the competitive position of their organization in the market. However, beyond commercial motives, they consider these changes a moral obligation. The organization simply cannot lag behind. An interviewee, for instance, states that "we need to act on corporate social responsibility. We should have a leading role. We need to have that intention. It needs to be part of our policy statement!" (p. 53).

2.5   DEEPENING THE THEORETICAL BASIS

The review of the literature indicates that responsibility and responsible leadership are central concepts in developing an understanding the characteristics of the eco-innovative and sustainable leader. Various sources in the literature elaborate on the feelings, behaviors and rationales of the sustainable leader of the future.

Waldman and Galvin (2008) argue that a responsible leader has to do more than just serve the shareholders and firm owners. Waldman and Galvin's (2008) responsible leader adopts a strategic and calculable method and, in addition, concentrates on dealing with social and societal issues. Such leaders think about how their managerial repertoire and style provides a positive return for the owners of the firm. To do this properly, the leaders apply a corporate monitoring and reward system that is control oriented. However, argue Waldman and Galvin (2008), serving shareholders and owners is not enough when someone wants to be a sustainably responsible leader. A responsible leader also serves all kinds of different stakeholders, and there can be many groups of stakeholders with an interest in the firm (see also Voegtlin, Patzer and Scherer, 2012). From this perspective, the leader may also serve employees, customers and the broader community. The responsible leader may need a strong sense of values concerning the needs and interests of this wide variety of stakeholder groups, as well as a sense for the noncalculable and unpredictable elements of decisions and outcomes. Most shareholders want return on investments, but other stakeholders want, for example, better working conditions, periodic information about the firm's investments in developing countries or its increased efforts to reduce its ecological footprint. Waldman and Galvin's (2008) view on responsible leadership addresses the strategic role of leaders in organizations. Sustainable leadership can be strategic. It can be both dedicated to serving both shareholders and stakeholders and oriented to the financial and societal impact of the leader's actions on behalf of the company. Waldman and Galvin's (2008) perspective takes into account that values cannot always be materialized, measured and calculated. To put it simply, the leader of sustainable innovation needs more competences than being an expert in finance. The responsible leader may also be capable of developing an overview of the stakeholders of the firm and their evolving demands, questions and needs. The responsible leader tries to serve these needs and tries to balance the interests of shareholders and stakeholders of the firm.

According to De Hoogh and Den Hartog (2008), a socially responsible leader feels an inner obligation "to do what is right." (S)he has self-control, knows what is right to do and takes responsibility for his/her own actions. De Hoogh and Den Hartog (2008) argue that a leader's social responsibility originates from personal attributes. A socially responsible leader has a so-called moral-legal standard of conduct. This means that the leader acts, decides and behaves because of a strong personal sense of what is good to do and what is not. The leader also feels an internal obligation to do well and to avoid wrong, bad or objectionable behavior. The responsible leader shows concern for others. In line with this, such a leader shows a concern about the consequences of actions and chooses to be accountable for behavior. The leader also evaluates and reflects on the actions undertaken and on the consequences of these actions. De Hoogh and Den Hartog (2008) describe the responsible leader as a person with an internal drive, operating according to emotional considerations and an internal system of ethical considerations. From this point of view, it can be argued that intrinsic processes in the body and mind of the person, including the leader's educational path, training and experience, have an effect on a leader's tendency to perform responsible leadership. De Hoogh and Den Hartog's (2008) model touches upon the psychological structures of behavior, on the degree to which responsibility is a personal trait and on the degree to which responsible leadership can be learned by means of education, training and experience. This psychological approach relates to all aspects of sustainable leadership that are drawn in this chapter and implies that a leader's charisma, management skills, strategic awareness, feel for people and contribution to a firm's societal impact are related to the leader's psychological structure and environment.

Fernando and Sim (2011) argue that a responsible manager needs to be assessed by others. They contend that assessment determines whether and to what degree a leader's behavior can be labeled "responsible." The outcomes of an assessment depend on the manager's results, the motives behind the behavior of the manager and the degree to which the manager did what she or he could be expected to do. This brings several new elements into the discussion about responsible leadership. It brings in the element of judgment, the criteria that are used to judge and the person or persons who judge the leader. This touches upon the difficulty, interpretability and subjective nature of responsible leadership. Maybe responsible leadership is not simply being charismatic, managerial, strategic and interactive or being aware of social and societal impact of actions. Maybe it is also a matter of judgment and personal taste. Fernando and Sim's (2011) responsible leader must be accountable. The responsible leader needs assessment and referents. The assessment process can change by the year, with continuously evolving moral, social, ethical and ecological standards and issues. Fernando and Sim (2011) argue that the broad and changing frame of reference that is used to assess relates to questions of evidence, intent and locus of responsibility and to the answers to these questions. Answers to questions of material evidence—that is, what the leader has done and what the consequences have been—can be examined to evaluate the leader's impact on stakeholders. The leader's responsible behavior can be examined through questions of intent, which examine the leader's intention behind behavior and decisions. A leader can also be judged on the basis of questions of locus of responsibility and on assessments of whether the leader has taken responsibility for the causes and effects of his or her actions, in a broader context and also including

Table 2.1   Frame of Reference for Eco-innovative and Sustainable Leadership

Leadership	Characteristics
Charisma	The leader has vision, energizes others, accelerates innovation, creates commitment, inspires, is intellectually stimulating, leads creative teams, binds people, has unconventional ideas, is flexible, is a role model, tells the story right, enhances team spirit, is innovation personified.
Control	The leader sets goals, establishes standards, defines roles, assigns responsibilities, measures progress, takes corrective action, plans projects, sets targets, assesses performance, rewards innovators, is accountable, knows what to control and to improve.
Strategy	The leader hires innovative personnel, invests in people, invests in innovation, integrates sustainability goals in the firm's strategy, has an innovation policy, serves shareholders, serves stakeholders.
Interaction	The leader empowers innovators, develops additional leadership, provides support, coaches people, guides people, shows individual consideration, communicates with stakeholders, involves others.
Societal impact	The leader is nature oriented, supports the environment, is trustworthy, is ethical, has a generational timeframe, builds communities, promotes long-term value, relies on cooperation, builds the firm's trustworthiness, considers the firm's position in the world, sets new societal standards and codes of conduct.

whether many others are in line for either praise or blame. The perspective of Fernando and Sim (2011) broadens the leadership element of the model of eco-innovation and sustainability management. It shows that it depends on evaluation schemes, on the persons who evaluate the leader and on the leader's results, including the degree to which the leader can be called a sustainable leader.

The research in this chapter indicates that leadership for eco-innovation and sustainability consists of a broad and comprehensive scheme of skills, activities, behaviors, attitudes, practices, traits, mentalities and intentions. It almost appears to be impossible for a leader to behave in all the ways the literature proposes. An overview of the characteristics of the ideal sustainable leader shows that such a leader is charismatic, has experience with management tools, is a smart strategist, knows people and creates a firm with a strong corporate societal position (see Table 2.1). Maybe that is too much to expect from one person. The overview in Table 2.1 can be seen as a frame of reference for possible behaviors, activities and considerations for sustainable leaders.

The research in this chapter indicates that the characteristics of sustainable leadership can contribute to the development of sustainably innovative ideas, concepts, visions and initiatives in industry.

2.6 SUMMARY

Leadership is the first element at the co-ideation level of the model of eco-innovation and sustainability management. The research shows that an eco-innovative leader can choose from a wide range of behaviors, styles and activities. The leader may need a certain degree of charisma to energize people toward new eco-innovative ambitions. The leader also may know how to apply management tools to plan and control the changes that are going to happen in the firm. Furthermore, an eco-innovative and sustainable leader can have a strategic vision and knows what direction the firm has to go and which stakeholders it has to serve. In addition to this, the leader may have a feel for people and know how to work with and among them. Finally, and not the least important, the leader can invest in creating and improving the firm's contribution to society. All these aspects of leadership can play a crucial role in firms and can contribute to the co-ideation processes in business. The sustainable leader develops the ideas and concepts that can grow into the sustainable products and services of the near future. He or she ideates in interaction and cooperation with stakeholders both inside as well as outside the firm. The sustainable leader can be an important person in the co-ideation process. The next important function in this co-ideation process is the entrepreneurial function. This is the subject of the next chapter.

3   Co-ideation by Entrepreneurs

3.1   INTRODUCTION

The second category of key players at the co-ideation level is the category of entrepreneurs. It is the category of people with a strong feeling for the creation and opening of new markets. The eco-innovative and sustainable entrepreneur is, more than other types of professionals, interested in sustainability as a means to generate value and to create markets, turnover and profits. The sustainable entrepreneur interprets sustainability primarily as a value driver; the entrepreneur knows that it can also be a cost driver but chooses to focus on it as a value driver. The sustainable entrepreneur needs to have the same characteristics as the more traditional entrepreneurial type but is distinguished by this belief in sustainability as a source of profit and wealth. Most entrepreneurs are keen on searching and finding new opportunities. They often focus on finding the latent desires of potential customers in markets that do not exist yet but that can emerge in the near future. They tend to look for chances and possibilities and try to develop new ideas for products, services and business models to serve new market segments. Entrepreneurs are aware of the fact that their propositions for new products, services and business processes have to be different from what already exists in the market. They thus try to develop ideas that are unique and, for example, supply or serve customers who are not served by competitors or who are located in neglected geographic areas. They offer products with distinctive features and designs that separate them from competitors in already existing markets. A sustainable entrepreneur needs the traits of any other entrepreneur and in addition concentrates on creating value, on opening markets and on developing new products, services and businesses that have sustainability as the core element that makes them unique and valuable. The sustainable entrepreneur is convinced that the social, sustainable and societal attributes of his or her new business propositions are valuable, that these are worth a price and that they will attract customers. Entrepreneurs are the second element at the co-ideation level of the model of eco-innovation and sustainability management (see Figure 3.1).

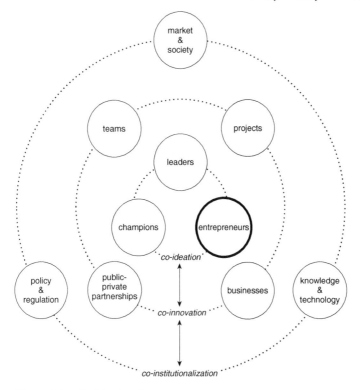

Figure 3.1   Co-ideation by entrepreneurs.

This chapter starts with an overview of theory that forms the basis of the entrepreneurship element of the model (Section 3.2). It continues with the methods used to further explore this element in practice and in theory (Section 3.3). It then explores the analytical value of the entrepreneurship element in practice (Section 3.4) and in theory (Section 3.5) and concludes with a summary of the main findings (Section 3.6).

3.2   THEORETICAL BASIS

The entrepreneurial function in business consists of many characteristics and comprises a complex of traits and behaviors that is not easy to perform. The sustainably conscious entrepreneur who wants to develop initiatives toward eco-innovation and sustainability has to be environmentally, socially and societally aware. Today's entrepreneurs act because they have a feel for emerging opportunities and for how to exploit these by creating unique ideas for new products and services. A sustainable entrepreneur needs all these traits, behaviors and skills and should also be able to see where economically fruitful propositions for new environmental, social or societal products, services and business emerge.

Opportunity

The entrepreneur initiates, drives and controls the innovation strategies and processes in the organization and takes the initiative to develop new products and services (Schumpeter, 1934). The entrepreneur is constantly looking for new ways to make money and always identifies new opportunities to sell products, smells where the opportunities are, launches crispy initiatives and projects and starts ventures to introduce products and services and to open markets (Beveridge and Guy, 2005). Stated boldly, the entrepreneur is driven by the possibilities of successful innovation and is not scared by the risks of failure (Dixon and Clifford, 2007; Klein Woolthuis, 2009). According to Burgelman, Christensen and Wheelwright (2004), there is more to entrepreneurship than the classic example of the enthusiastic individual with the start-up venture. A lot of entrepreneurship is going on in firms that already exist. Entrepreneurial individuals, for example, often work for incumbent—that is, large, powerful and leading—firms. The entrepreneurial issue in these incumbents is how to use the initiatives of entrepreneurial employees and to provide them the possibilities to develop their entrepreneurial propositions for the benefit of the firm. When an entrepreneur's initiatives are considered very important, these can be integrated directly into the firm's business processes and market activities. It is also an option for incumbent companies to establish a new product or service development department or to create a special business unit. This means that entrepreneurs create organizations by starting one for themselves or for the firms they work for.

Creation

According to Williams and McGuire (2010), a main driver of national economic growth is related to the creativity of the nation's entrepreneurs. Although this statement is often posited and supported by many sources in the literature, the question remains how incumbent firms can stimulate and monitor the development of innovative ideas by their entrepreneurial employees. Williams and McGuire (2010) contend that firms' entrepreneurial activity can be evaluated by using measures such as, for example, the number of patents and publications the firm's employees realize. Patents and publications are an indicator of a nation's economic creativity. Patents codify the creation, retention and transfer of knowledge. Publications capture the knowledge that is gathered, used, transformed and further developed by people in companies, universities and commercial laboratories. While patents and publications can be measured and are an indicator of the entrepreneurial activity of an organization, R&D spending is another indicator of innovation and entrepreneurial activity. Williams and McGuire (2010) write that "R&D spending may reflect an organization's ability to identify, absorb, and improve on technologies and know-how in order to maximize competitive advantage" (p. 401). R&D spending can also have a positive effect on other indicators of innovation creation by a firm's entrepreneurs, such as trademarks and license fees. Commercialization of intellectual property in the form of trademarks and license fees can lead to an increase of revenues for companies. Williams and McGuire (2010) also maintain that the activity of independent entrepreneurs who have their own firms can also contribute to a nation's innovativeness and mention a country's self-employment rates as another indicator of its innovativeness. Self-employment rates can be an indicator of the number of independently organized entrepreneurs in a country. These people choose or are forced to open and serve markets on their own, for themselves, and with unique business proposals.

Uniqueness

Wu, Chang and Chen (2008) establish that a firm's intellectual capital can be one of the main sources of enduring competitive advantage. Firms that hire employees with a lot of knowledge and intellectual capacity may receive, as a return on their investment in knowledge and creativity, more and better innovation than competitors that do not invest in a knowledgeable workforce. Knowledge workers can be key persons in an entrepreneurial firm and can be capable of developing unique proposals for new products, services and combinations of these. According to Berkhout, Hartmann and Trott (2010), knowledge workers link product creation activities with customer demand. Knowledge workers combine the latest, state-of-the-art knowledge from science and engineering with a strong commitment to and an understanding of new and unique emerging markets. They are aware of both the technological developments in science and industry and the new topics, issues, fads and trends in society and consumer markets. This combination of technological and societal awareness can make them outstanding creators of unique business propositions. The entrepreneurial knowledge worker confronts and aligns knowledge and insights from both technological evolution and market dynamics and can trigger a continuous process of creating new propositions for new products and services, with the potential to serve emerging markets and latent consumer needs.

Economic Awareness

York and Venkataraman (2010) contend that entrepreneurial activity can be highly capable of addressing environmental issues and that those issues represent a new type of opportunity that entrepreneurs are going to tackle in the coming years. York and Venkataraman (2010) suggest that the current less or nonsustainable way of producing, selling, buying and using products will come to an end and that society is ready for new firms with alternative eco-innovative and sustainable ideas and new people who identify with these ideas. York and Venkataraman (2010) substantiate that a for-profit sphere, that is, the presence of economic chances to generate turnover with eco-innovative and sustainable business and make a profit, can become the solution to rising sustainability problems. Differences in market prices and possible profits can be the triggers for new innovative entrepreneurial activity. In line with York and Venkataraman (2010), Schaltegger and Wagner (2011) agree that economic awareness can be an important characteristic of an effective sustainable entrepreneur. It means that the sustainable entrepreneur has the ability to envision the market potential of ideas for sustainable products and services. Schaltegger and Wagner (2011) contend that entrepreneurship can contribute to the solving of environmental problems and at the same time create economic value for all that are involved. A main challenge is thus to balance environmental and economic parameters and to generate more money and value than respectively spent and destroyed. Schaltegger and Wagner (2011) distinguish three types of sustainably conscious entrepreneurs. The first type of entrepreneur wants to solve societal problems and does not want to make a profit per se. This entrepreneurial type is satisfied when the money balance is in equilibrium, which means that the same amount of money goes in and out of the firm each month. A second type of entrepreneur is the entrepreneur who knows that regulatory, societal and market institutions need to change to enable profitable or economically healthy sustainable initiatives. Such an entrepreneur is mainly developing projects and activities that stimulate institutional decision makers to change the rules, incentives, laws and penalties in the economic system. A third category of entrepreneurs wants to contribute to solving societal and environmental problems by building a successful business and by creating sustainable development through new corporate initiatives. This type of entrepreneurs' main challenge is to start with a small contribution to sustainable development and to turn this into a large contribution that grows and changes industry and society.

3.3   RESEARCH METHOD

Additional empirical and theoretical studies are carried out to further increase the analytical value of the entrepreneurship element of the model of eco-innovation and sustainability management for industry.

Step 1.   Shaping the Research Model

This chapter builds on the results from the initial study of Bossink (2011a) (see Appendix 1). It focuses on the entrepreneurship element of the model (Section 3.2) and conducts exploratory empirical research in various Dutch industries to investigate how the entrepreneurship element of the model holds for other empirical contexts (Section 3.4). A review of the literature on eco-innovation management is carried out to explore how this element can be shaped to claim a broader analytical value for industry (Section 3.5).

Step 2.   Conducting Theoretical and Empirical Studies

Literature databases are consulted for research papers on entrepreneurship in the area of ecological, green, social, societal, environmental and biological business. In addition to this, ten managers and experts in various industries in the Netherlands are interviewed and asked to reflect on the question of what sustainability issues they think are important for their business (Klawer, 2008).

Step 3.   Analyzing and Synthesizing the Studies' Outcomes

The entrepreneurship element in the initial model (Bossink, 2011a) is confronted with the additional empirical and theoretical studies. On the basis of the outcomes of this analysis, the characteristics of the entrepreneurship element at the co-ideation level are defined for industry (Section 3.5).

3.4   EXPLORING THE EMPIRICAL FIELD

The interviewees confirm that all forms of entrepreneurship can have a positive effect on eco-innovation and sustainability in industry. The exploratory interviews indicate that an entrepreneur's opportunity-seeking behavior, positive attitude toward creation and being creative, an ongoing drive to create unique business propositions and an awareness of economic feasibility of new sustainable initiatives can be main elements of eco-innovative and sustainable entrepreneurship. This section is the author's interpretation of Klawer (2008), and quotations are taken from that source.

Opportunity

In the past years, it became a normal economic practice in industry to use resources as if they are free. Labor and capital are invested in mining fossil resources and natural materials, but in the economic system the natural resources itself are considered to be abundant and available for unlimited use. Nowadays it seems that this century-spanning tradition is changing. Today, industry increasingly understands that natural resources, either for energy or for materials, are neither infinitely usable nor reusable. Over the past decades, society and business became aware of the earth's limits; they understand that the use of natural resources comes at a cost and that this cost can be taken into consideration and can be made part of the business system.

Economies and businesses are increasingly aware that they can incorporate the costs of use, ownership, reuse, contamination, toxicity and environmental change into businesses' production systems. Because industrialized countries start to integrate the eco-costs in their economies and production systems, unsustainable businesses are becoming more expensive and sustainable businesses more economically viable. In this respect, in the interviews, the representatives of provincial authorities stress the importance of new regulations and national policy. They want to offer more opportunities for entrepreneurs to sell ecological or sustainable products and services, for example by directly buying from sustainable suppliers themselves. As one of the representatives of a provincial authority commented: "When we, on all governmental levels, focus on purchasing sustainable products, the demand and supply for sustainable products will increase. . . . We stimulate that entrepreneurs can develop an interest in sustainable production" (p. 54). Another representative of a provincial authority talks about helping entrepreneurs to become aware of the cost reductions that are possible: "There are two options to stimulate sustainable entrepreneurship. One: repressive, which means that rules, taxes and fines are applied. Two: we believe that it is better to be positive, to increase entrepreneurs' awareness of the importance of sustainability and to let them realize that it can also reduce costs" (p. 55). The interviews indicate that some entrepreneurs start to discover the opportunities of sustainable business.

Creation

The interviewees agree that entrepreneurs have to cooperate with others, such as consultancy firms, research institutes, governmental agencies, or even competing firms, to create eco-innovative and sustainable products and services. In other words, "No man is an island." Sustainable initiatives can become successful and can evolve from a small business into something big, but, say the interviewees, always by cooperating with counterparts, by trying, failing and succeeding with others in the same or in adjacent areas, never in isolation. The government is aware of this and invests in bringing together entrepreneurs who want to start a new sustainable business. One of the interviewees, employed by the provincial government, stresses the importance of organizing meetings: "We organize seminars where entrepreneurs can learn from sustainable entrepreneurs. We are also committed to bringing several companies together; Companies that can inform and help one another in terms of sustainability and technological development" (p. 57). The respondents all mention the entrepreneurial role as essential in the process of transforming industry from a resource-consuming industry into a resource-preserving industry. Although it is often said that a characteristic trait of an entrepreneur is that he or she is a loner who is determined to achieve personal goals, most respondents' answers indicate that cooperation, openness, dialogue and exchange of experience and knowledge with others may be a key feature of successful entrepreneurship in the field of eco-innovation and sustainability.

Uniqueness

Several respondents remark that sustainability is an aspect of business that can enable firms to create a unique image in the marketplace. Nevertheless, they are also uncertain about the aforementioned cooperative aspect of eco-innovative and sustainable business creation. The interviews show a paradoxical picture. On the one hand, entrepreneurs and entrepreneurial firms want to be unique and refuse to share their unique knowledge and capabilities with others or other companies. On the other hand, sustainable innovation dynamics require them to cooperate with and open up to other firms. A respondent of a production company that strives for uniqueness puts this as follows: a governmental agency "suggested that we could cooperate with another firm. We do not want that! . . . We want exclusivity with this product. One of the major reasons for us to start developing this product is competitive advantage. That is something we do not want to give away" (p. 60). A university researcher uses a comparable line of reasoning when he states: "Small and medium sized enterprises can use their 'personal touch' as a unique selling point, and this includes sustainable development. . . . Dutch small and medium sized enterprises are very careful when it comes to cooperation. This is because they do not want to give away business processes to other firms" (p. 65). The key belief among interviewees is that aligning business processes, sharing information and knowledge and bundling strengths with other firms can be a threat and that it is difficult to turn this threat into an opportunity. The interviewees confirm that although cooperation can be a main key to the development of eco-innovative and sustainable products and services, their main goal remains to create sustainable competitive advantage on their own and not in partnerships. Their preference is not to cooperate, not to share ideas, not to share knowledge and not to join multiparty teams and projects. When that is impossible, they start to look for opportunities to cooperate with others.

Economic Awareness

Most respondents think that sustainability *can* go hand in hand with profitability. They stress the word "can" because they are all aware of the difficulties of turning an eco-innovative idea into a profitable business. Although they see opportunities for sustainable business, they also realize that sustainability and profit are not synonyms. An entrepreneur working for a commercial company in a business-to-business setting, for example, comments: "My customers all require my products to carry an eco-certificate. In my opinion this just costs a lot of time and money and it has absolutely no additional value. . . . In fact, these requirements influence the entire supply chain . . . it increases the costs, but also requires costly organizational and operational changes in the production facilities" (p. 62). With respect to this, a consultant says that helping firms to implement sustainability and supporting them in cooperating with counterparts are not extremely profitable yet: "In the first phase I . . . describe the initial idea. In the second phase, we experiment together with universities, the government and knowledge institutions and test the feasibility of the project. In the final phase contractors get involved and the project starts. In that third phase I start to make money as an advisor" (p. 66). Nevertheless, some interviewees see glimmers of light in the darkness and foresee increasing economic perspectives. A respondent from a research center, for example, stresses that sustainability can have the potential of being a value driver instead of a cost driver and that it is important to start analyzing what the actual benefits of sustainable initiatives can be: "Making use of new technological or other knowledge in a product, service or organization in order to add value to the total supply chain must be envisaged. For a company this means competitive advantage and higher profits" (p. 63). The interviews indicate that sustainable business may become widespread and profitable but has a long way to go.

3.5   DEEPENING THE THEORETICAL BASIS

The review of the literature shows that balancing and optimizing sustainability and profitability is an important goal for the eco-innovative and sustainable entrepreneur. Sources in the literature stress that this balancing act is not easy and requires much perseverance.

Shepherd and Patzelt (2010) define sustainable entrepreneurship as a function that "is focused on the preservation of nature, life support, and community in the pursuit of perceived opportunities to bring into existence future products, processes, and services for gain, where gain is broadly construed to include economic and non-economic gains to individuals, the economy, and society" (p. 142). Their definition builds on two concepts: "sustainable" and "development." Shepherd and Patzelt (2010) contend that the sustainable entrepreneur wants to sustain the earth, biodiversity and ecosystems, aims to preserve the environment and natural resources and strives to protect communities and relationships between people. These communities and people share meaning, stories, norms, history and identity, and this is also part of the world that needs to be sustained. The aspects of sustainability Shepherd and Patzelt (2010) mention exceed the scope of traditional economic reasoning and of contemporary business. Shepherd and Patzelt (2010) do not close their eyes to the traditional financial aspects of business and trade and argue that the sustainable entrepreneur should enable economic gain for actors and for society. However, they do not apply a unilateral financial approach and take the noneconomic gains to individuals and society into account, including in education, health and life expectancy. Shepherd and Patzelt's (2010) arguments support the entrepreneurship element that is proposed in the model of eco-innovation and sustainability. Their argument touches upon the "opportunity-seeking behavior" of the entrepreneur and investigates the characteristics of a society, of consumer markets and of institutional contexts that prepare for a future that demands an increase in sustainability. In addition to this, they emphasize "creative competence" as an important entrepreneurial trait and stress that it can be the entrepreneur who develops economic and noneconomic gains for individuals in industry and society. This directly relates to the proposed "economic awareness" of the sustainable entrepreneur.

Dixon and Clifford (2007) apply a somewhat different line of reasoning from Shepherd and Patzelt (2010). Dixon and Clifford (2007) argue that a sustainable entrepreneur's main goal may be to deliver social value and that economic value is a welcome by-product. Many traditional entrepreneurs may prefer to put these two aspects of sustainable business in reverse order, but the sustainable entrepreneur is convinced that extra environmental, social or societal content in a product or service has the potential to generate extra incomes. The basic concept behind this belief is that the consumer will pay an extra amount of money as long as producers are able to transparently explain what the extra sustainable features of their products and services are and how they improve quality. What makes Dixon and Clifford's (2007) argument interesting, specifically to the research in this chapter on the entrepreneurship element, is that it provides an alternative to people in business, government, research centers and institutional organizations who say that eco-business just costs money. Dixon and Clifford's (2007) alternatives are quality specifications, quality perceptions and quality management. When companies, authorities and institutions are able to specify the sustainable qualities of their products and of their intangible processes and services, they may ask and receive higher prices for their merchandise.

Although a lot of knowledge of entrepreneurship in general and sustainable entrepreneurship in particular are already available, many questions remain unanswered, and many issues are open for further research. Recently, Dacin, Dacin and Tracy (2011) published a research agenda with interesting research questions in the area of social entrepreneurship. They suggest five possible avenues for future research. Their first proposed line of research fits with the arguments of Shepherd and Patzelt (2010) and Dixon and Clifford (2007). This first proposed line of research addresses the question of how social entrepreneurs understand and manage the conflict of the for-profit and nonprofit logics of their actions. In addition, Dacin, Dacin and Tracy (2011) aim to broaden the research domain and also incorporate research questions from a different, more psychological and social point of view. One new line of research that they propose is to investigate the networks of the social entrepreneurs. This means that the subjects of study will be the local

Table 3.1   Frame of Reference for Eco-innovative and Sustainable Entrepreneurship

Entrepreneurship	Characteristics
Opportunity	The entrepreneur seeks market opportunities, finds market opportunities, exploits market opportunities, serves new markets, starts ventures, creates organizations, develops new products and services, thinks sustainability is future business, expects sustainability to be a driver of market growth.
Creation	The entrepreneur develops economic and noneconomic gains, develops patents, publishes, owns trademarks, receives royalties and license fees, is self-employed, has an independent position as an entrepreneur in an incumbent firm, co-creates, acts in a large social network.
Uniqueness	The entrepreneur is a knowledge worker, connects technology and markets, knows about the latest technological developments, knows about the latest trends in the market, is aware of societal issues, cooperates with others and other firms and organizations.
Economic awareness	The entrepreneur balances sustainable and economic gains and constraints, sees sustainability as the basic driver of economic growth, considers sustainability to be a value driver, does not close his or her eyes for the costs of eco-innovation and sustainability, markets sustainability as a quality aspect that is worth the money.

networks in which sustainable entrepreneurs set up their initiatives, as well as the virtual networks that enable them to build communities and rapidly share their ideas. Another prospective line of research Dacin, Dacin and Tracy (2011) introduce is to study the culture of social entrepreneurship and to focus on the rituals that are used to recognize and honor eco- and socio-preneurs, such as awards and recognitions for social heroes. They propose a line of research that interprets the mystifications of social entrepreneurs' successes, which legitimizes the sustainable entrepreneur as an important person in business and society. This relates to the fourth proposed line of inquiry, which is the study of the sustainable entrepreneur's heroic identity and brand quality. Finally, a fifth line of research is the line of entrepreneurial cognition, that is, whether the social entrepreneur thinks and behaves differently from other entrepreneurs. Dacin, Dacin and Tracey's (2011) research agenda can be a starting point for a broader and deeper insight into the traits and behaviors of the sustainable entrepreneur.

The research in this chapter indicates that entrepreneurship for eco-innovation and sustainability is a profession with many characteristic traits and behaviors. The literature describes more traits, behaviors, approaches and guidelines than a single entrepreneur can apply. An overview of the characteristics of the sustainable entrepreneur shows that such people seek, find and exploit opportunities, create ideas for unique business propositions and balance and optimize sustainable and economic goals (see Table 3.1). The overview can be seen as a frame of reference, not a prescription, for entrepreneurial behavior in favor of eco-innovation and sustainability.

The research in this chapter indicates that the characteristics of sustainable entrepreneurship can contribute to the development of sustainably innovative ideas, concepts, visions and initiatives in industry.

3.6 SUMMARY

Entrepreneurship is the second element at the co-ideation level of the model of eco-innovation and sustainability management. The research shows that the behavioral repertoire of the sustainable entrepreneur is capacious. The sustainable entrepreneur has a strong sense for opportunities and for developing ideas for profitable new sustainable businesses and organizations. The sustainable entrepreneur creates business prospects and new ideas for products and services and knows what is needed to be a unique provider of sustainable goods in new and in existing markets. The sustainable entrepreneur balances economic and sustainable revenues and costs and forms ideas in cooperation and interaction with various stakeholders of the firm. The sustainable entrepreneur can be an important person in the co-ideation process. The third important person at the co-ideation level is the champion of sustainable innovation, which is the subject of the next chapter.

4 Co-ideation by Champions

4.1 INTRODUCTION

The third category of key players at the co-ideation level is the category of champions. This category comprises those who have the intrinsic drive to innovate, the people who are highly motivated to create new things and who walk and talk innovation all the time. The champion of eco-innovation and sustainability is more interested than others in renewal, in innovation and in rejuvenation. Such a champion is capable of getting the subject on the agenda of the managers of the company. The champion of innovation is often seen as the central person in the innovation process with an above-average intention to create, renew and change. A champion of innovation is a walking advertisement for continuous improvement and innovation, is tireless in conceiving new ideas and does not rest until these are realized. A champion is the person who probably has more ideas than can be realized and is a source of information for others on how the business could be changed or completely turned around. The champion is also an accumulator of knowledge, is interested in everything and anyone and continuously gathers and transmits information. This information-seeking and -sharing behavior forms a valuable source of knowledge for the company. Champions of sustainable innovation are needed to create a sustainably innovative culture in an organization. They infect others with their new ideas on social, societal, ecological and sustainable affairs. In addition, they are drivers of companywide discussions about value creation for stakeholders and society. The champion of innovation is the third element at the co-ideation level of the model of eco-innovation and sustainability management (see Figure 4.1).

This chapter introduces the theory that forms the basis of the sustainable champion element of the model (Section 4.2). It continues with the methods used to explore the analytical validity of the element for industry (Section 4.3). It then explores the analytical value of the champion element in practice (Section 4.4) and in theory (Section 4.5). The chapter concludes with a summary of the main findings (Section 4.6).

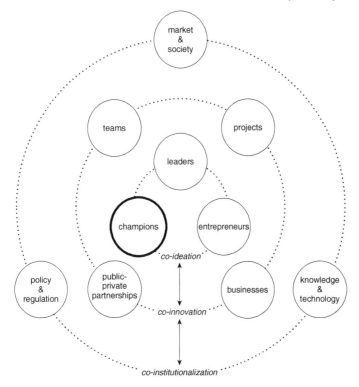

Figure 4.1　Co-ideation by champions.

4.2　THEORETICAL BASIS

The role of innovation champion is a role that can be performed by all sorts of employees. Innovation champion is not a job or a job title. Everybody can be a champion of innovation, and this means that, for example, production workers, managers, the chief executive officer and the financial specialists of the firm all can behave like champions of eco- and sustainable innovation. Innovation champions can be described as hobbyists, enthusiasts, visionaries, gurus, experts and oracles who are intrinsically motivated to create new businesses, products and markets. The word "champion" is not part of their job description; neither does the company explicitly expect people to be champions of innovation. A champion of sustainable innovation can be a company's main promoter of renewal because of an intrinsic drive to change and renew. The innovation champion likes to meet with and talk to people and hear about what is new and what issues the company can deal with in the coming times. The champion of eco-innovation and sustainability thinks that it is important to integrate sustainable innovation into the business processes of the firm.

Promoter

The champion of innovation persuades others to join the innovation process and tries as hard and talks as long as needed to convince top managers, middle-level managers, specialists and other direct colleagues that new things are happening, are going to happen or need to be happening in and around the firm. This champion proclaims that it is important to introduce a new product or a new service or to consider an alteration of the production process. The champion knows the ins and outs of the innovations that she or he proclaims and likes to delve into the details. The champion often is a lobbyist and has a strong and large network of associates, above-average status in the organization and always one or two good ideas in mind. The champion talks to others about these ideas all the time and hopes that they are adopted. When the ideas are adopted, the champion joins the innovation process and starts realizing the idea (Hauschildt and Kirchmann, 2001). Gemünden, Salomo and Hölzle (2007) studied the roles of innovation champions in innovation projects and argue that a promoting champion "supports the project above-average" (p. 412). A champion of innovation can use several sources of power to promote innovation or an innovation project, including his or her hierarchical position, knowledge base or position in the social network of the company. The champion can use personal expertise and "promote the project by his/her high technological know-how" (p. 412). The champion can use personal knowledge of the firm's business processes, "act as a link between decision makers and experts" (p. 412), use personal knowledge of the network of firms that surrounds the company and "support the search for external cooperation partners" (p. 412). Gemünden, Salomo and Hölzle (2007) argue that a promoting champion of innovation is not necessarily a "hero" who wins where everybody else fails or who walks on while others quit when the champion is put to the test or encounters opposition. According to Gemünden, Salomo and Hölzle (2007), today's promoter is perhaps not that hero but a normal person with the capability to find out what the main options and potential risks are and then finds ways to realize the options without too many failures.

Inventor

A champion can also be an inventor who has knowledge and transforms knowledge into ideas for innovative products and services. Such as person can be a designer who makes blueprints for new products, an industrial engineer who conceives ideas for new production plants or an industrial marketer who develops strategies for the firm to conquer new markets. All these types of innovation champions may have new ideas, new knowledge, the drive to gain new knowledge and the creativity to transform knowledge into inventions (Hauschildt and Kirchmann, 2001; Howell and Boies, 2004). Andersson and Berggren (2007) argue that champions contribute to three important and mutually supportive invention processes. First, champions' ideas can be drivers of the development of patents. The development of patents requires a lot of knowledge and time from the champion of innovation, as well as sufficient funding from the company or from external investors. Second, the champions' ideas can be drivers of the development of new products. In the process of new-product development, the innovation champion has to work with many colleagues to realize the innovative ideas. New-product development demands intensive cooperation among designers, production engineers and marketers as they adjust product specifications, production organization and capacity and respond to market demands, sales forecasts and expected trends. Third, champions' ideas can be drivers of the development of a company's technological competences. The ideas can trigger an organization to continuously innovate and can add to the innovative capabilities of the firm. Andersson and Berggren (2007) argue that the inventive activities of champions contribute to the innovativeness of the firm.

Gatekeeper

The gatekeeping champion gathers and processes information about changes in the organization and the outside world. The champion of innovation traces potentially useful knowledge from inside and outside the firm and tries to get this knowledge applied in the firm. The gatekeeping champion has access to information that others do not have. This kind of champion has a hunger for knowledge and can have a strong and large network of contacts. The drive of the innovation champion to obtain knowledge originates in an intrinsic desire to know, to watch new trends and to share knowledge with colleagues. The gatekeeping champion keeps the organization informed (Fleming and Waguespack, 2007; Rothaermel and Hess, 2007). According to MacDonald and Piekkari (2005), who studied the characteristics of the personal networks of champions, gatekeeping activity is not always as productive and valuable as imagined. MacDonald and Piekkari (2005) contend that not all leaders and managers can handle the increasing power and freedom of gatekeeping champions in the groups they are supposed to lead. A gatekeeping champion's information networks can evade a leader or manager's control. An innovation manager needs gatekeepers because of their access to knowledge and information, but this goes on the expense of the manager's sense of control. When organizations' managers try to control the knowledge networks of gatekeepers and claim that the gatekeeper's knowledge belongs to the firm or when organizations permit champions limited access to and interaction with the outside world, the information-gathering and knowledge-producing function of champions is under pressure. A major conclusion MacDonald and Piekkari (2005) draw is therefore that not all collaboration projects with firms and institutes that are set up to freely share information and develop new knowledge are successful. They contend that relationships among people in a collaboration program can even be "pale and flaccid." They plead for intensive gatekeeping dynamics, which means extra openness and freedom for gatekeeping champions to interact and explore where the opportunities are.

Integrator

Another characteristic of a champion of innovation is the champion's capability to integrate sustainability in the operations of the company. The champion of innovation understands that the integration of sustainability into the design of new products and services can change a firm into a sustainable firm. Design practices are an important means to an innovative end. According to Casey (2009), a champion of sustainable innovation needs to invest in positive social and environmental impacts of designs, design processes and the production processes. (For more about the methodology of eco-innovative and sustainable product design, see Appendix 6.) She refers to the so-called Designers Accord in which an association of more than 100,000 designers defines the essentials of sustainable creation and design. An important principle of the Designers Accord is that a sustainable firm needs to engage in an ongoing conversation with its clients and customers about the integration of sustainable alternatives into industrial designs. It must create a "real world and on-line network that enables conversation about opportunities and challenges in creating sustainable products, services and businesses" (p. 62). Casey (2009) argues that potential champions of sustainable innovation who aim to integrate sustainability in their organization must participate in the sustainable design movement. They have the responsibility to train their teams and teach or show their teams what the ecological footprint of their work is. They have to advance "the understanding of environmental and social issues from a design perspective by actively contributing to the communal knowledge base for sustainable design" (p. 63); in other words, according to Rosenberg (2004), they should contribute to the "widespread integration of corporate social environmental responsibility principles . . . [that become] . . . part of the mainstream operating values of the organization" (p. 8).

4.3   RESEARCH METHOD

Additional theoretical studies are performed to further increase the analytical value of the champion element of the model of eco-innovation and sustainability management for industry.

Step 1.   Shaping the Research Model

This chapter builds on the results from the initial study of Bossink (2011a) (see Appendix 1). It focuses on the champion element of the model (Section

4.2). It conducts empirical research in the Dutch building industry to exemplify the champion element of the model (Section 4.4) and presents a literature review that further explores how the champion element can be shaped toward a broader analytical value for industry (Section 4.5).

Step 2. Conducting Theoretical and Empirical Studies

Literature databases are consulted for research papers on championship for environmental, ecological, green, social, societal, biological and sustainable innovations in business, firms and industry. In addition to this, six managers and experts in the Dutch building industry are interviewed and asked to reflect on the sustainability issues related to sustainable innovation championship. Their activities are observed in innovation projects in which they either act as an innovation champion or are assisted by an innovation champion (Bossink, 2011a).

Step 3. Analyzing and Synthesizing the Studies' Outcomes

The champion element in the initial model (Bossink, 2011a) is confronted with the additional theoretical study. On the basis of the outcomes of this analysis, the characteristics of the champion element at the co-ideation level of the model are articulated for industry (Section 4.5).

4.4   EXPLORING THE EMPIRICAL FIELD

The interviews and observations confirm that all forms of championship can have a positive effect on eco-innovation and sustainability in industry. The exploratory interviews indicate that a champion of innovation's tendency to promote innovative ideas, to be in the center of multiple social networks inside and outside the company, and the champion's intrinsic drive to integrate sustainability in the firm's business processes and product and service portfolio can have a crucial influence on sustainable innovation. This section is taken from Bossink (2011a: 46–50). It describes three cases in which champions of eco- and sustainable innovation try to develop, design and realize creative ideas and solutions in the field of sustainable building.

Promoter

A designer from an architect's firm had to draw and materialize a design for a sustainable urban area. This specialist turned out to be a promoter of sustainability. He had years of experience in creating sustainable urban design. Already while studying architecture at university, he specialized in sustainable design. In the next twenty-five years of his career, he gained much experience in this field. In the innovation project, he completed the basic design for the sustainable urban plan quite quickly, after only two months. The architect spent the remaining fifteen months of the project on promoting sustainability in general and his own design in particular. In every meeting with city officials and real estate developers, he took and was allowed to take much time to talk. In a ninety-minute meeting, he always gave a presentation of at least thirty minutes. In these presentations, he described the characteristics of his sustainable urban plans. His goal was to inform and convince the other members of the team that the green aspects of the design had both technical and commercial quality. He presented several green elements, such as "parcels that allow living rooms to be situated on the sunny side, . . . frequent use of green areas where animals can live and move . . . [and] restrictions for motorized traffic that are in favor of pedestrians and cyclists" (p. 46). His approach was effective. He convinced many people of the importance of sustainability and they approved his plans.

Inventor

In another building project, one of the city officials turned out to be an inventing champion. He wanted to design a system for sustainable water management. Throughout the project, his supervising project leader supported his work. The inventor designed a system of water collection, storage and disposal that was based on the wadi concept. A wadi is a hydrological system in which water is collected in narrow, shallow channels that crisscross the area. The inventor told the attendees at meetings that "all went well" but paid little attention to providing specific information to the team members. His work was too specialized and experimental, and the inventor was not an outgoing person. He wanted to concentrate on his work. The project manager was very confident in his skills and gave him every opportunity to perfect his work. Eventually, the wadi system was completely integrated into the design for a new urban area. This project shows that a champion who has no promoting qualities at all but who owns a surplus of invention skills can be a significant driver of innovation in an innovation project.

Gatekeeper and Integrator

In another case, a designer from a consultancy firm had to coordinate the design and development of an ecological garden in which several houses were situated. The designer acted as both a gatekeeper and an integrator. Everything he did was aimed at gathering, exchanging and applying knowledge and information about sustainability. At the start of the project, it was not clear what the specific objectives were. The concept of sustainability was not specified, and the team members were asked to specify it themselves. The designer chose to involve all participating officials and commercial parties in generating ideas for the eco-garden. He spent a lot of time getting everybody involved in the design process. First, he organized a design meeting with colleagues from his own office. He asked them to brainstorm about the sustainability aspects to be included in the plan. He used the outcomes of this meeting to make two different sketches, which he then presented to the members of the project. He asked them to brainstorm on additional and conflicting ideas. One of the municipal officials had so many ideas that she was invited to visit the designer's office, an invitation that she accepted. The principal designer used this brainstorming session to improve the two drafts. Again, these were presented to the project team, and members were asked to choose one of the drafts. The team discussed the options for more than three hours but could not choose between them. Both designs were rated as good and beautiful. The project leader decided to ask the designer to create a preliminary and final design in which the best aspects of the two sketches were combined, which he did. He had, as he said himself, "made a design with green boundaries, shells for walkways, trees with edible fruit and plenty of room for animals to nest themselves" (p. 48). The designer's approach led to a joint design that evoked great enthusiasm among the participants. The designer made a final design using the input on sustainable affairs from a team of fifteen specialists.

4.5   DEEPENING THE THEORETICAL BASIS

The review of the literature indicates that the efforts of the champion of innovation to integrate sustainability into the processes of the company and into the designs of the company's products and services are a distinctive characteristic of this special person.

Soosay (2005) argues that champions of innovation are characterized by openness to organizational change. They have the capability to look across the boundaries of the company. Today's business increasingly demands that companies intensively cooperate with other firms in the supply and production chain. This often means that cooperating firms work with joint planning and information systems. This can be a challenge and is often difficult, but the champion knows that an investment in these cooperative arrangements and systems can result in improved business processes on a larger scale. Champions of innovation are aware of the potential benefits that come from joint investments in the supply and production chain. Soosay (2005) argues that persons who perform the role of innovation champion must be eager learners with flexible minds. These characteristics are necessary to gain deep and up-to-date insight into the direction of today's and future consumer demands. The innovation champion has to understand the basic needs of the customers and must also know what aesthetic and functional trends influence customers' demands. A champion needs an open mind in order to be able to receive today's unique customer requests. Such flexibility and adaptability are enabled by an open and learning-oriented attitude, which in turn enables the champion of innovation to share information and knowledge across functional, departmental company boundaries.

These behaviors enable value creation on the level of the supply and production chain. Soosay (2005) argues that this kind of cross-boundary communication is needed to create value between functions and firms. This is in line with the function of the innovation champion at the co-ideation level of the model of eco-innovation and sustainability management. It further stresses the importance of champions who neglect boundaries and look only at the possibilities of cooperative innovation. They do not bother too much about the impediments.

People sometimes tend to overrate the character, behavior and traits of the persons who play the role of champion. With respect to this, Bissola and Imperatori (2011) argue that creativity and creative genius are often mystified and that many clichés circulate in practice. Bissola and Imperatori (2011) contend that many beliefs about creativity among managers and other practitioners are rather naïve but still widespread. One of these widespread beliefs that these authors doubt is that "creativity is a matter of talent" (p. 86). They maintain that professionals with a small or average set of creative skills and traits can become creative if they are given a well-designed organizational setting or project organization in which to work. In addition to that, Bissola and Imperatori (2011) argue that a group of highly creative individuals is not necessarily creative as a group because of possible conflicts, conflicting interests and communication problems. Another cliché they highlight is that "creativity needs boundless time and sources of inspiration" (p. 86). Bissola and Imperatori (2011) assert the opposite and state that time pressure can be a real stimulator of innovation, for example in situations where firms want to develop innovations more efficiently and effectively. The next creativity belief they question is that "creative genius needs to feel free" (p. 86). They argue that rules and work specialization do not have to stifle creativity at all and even can enhance creativity, "especially in groups composed of low-level creative people" (p. 86). Rules can have a structuring effect on the innovation process and help to translate ideas into results that fit with the organizational goals. Another idea about creativity Bissola and Imperatori (2011) challenge and label as naïve is that "a positive climate supports creativity" (p. 86). They argue that a good team climate can also distract people from being creative. In groups with highly creative people, time and goal awareness are often relatively low, and there is a risk that the project will have a good atmosphere but fail to deliver. With respect to the aspects of championship that are presented in this chapter, the clichés rebutted by Bissola and Imperatori (2011) emphasize that having champions on board of an organization or project is not a guarantee of success or results. Champions can even have a negative effect on the innovative process. Bissola and Imperatori (2011) contend that there is a reasonable chance that a team that works with one or more competent champions will fail because people have different interests, speak different languages or on a basic level do not want to work with one another. We can conclude here that Bissola and Imperatori (2011) weaken the assumption that it is

Table 4.1 Frame of Reference for Eco-innovative and Sustainable Championship

Championship	Characteristics
Promoter	The champion persuades others to innovate, lobbies to get innovation on the agenda, talks about innovation all the time, connects people, ideas and resources, convinces colleagues, is an advocate of innovation, is an effective and calculating innovator, has experience with innovation, is well educated in the subjects (s)he talks about.
Inventor	The champion generates ideas, generates creativity, creates knowledge, is the engine behind the development of firms' technological capabilities, is a designer, is a builder, is an engineer, is the driver of the creation of patents, new products and services.
Gatekeeper	The champion traces knowledge, shares knowledge, looks for trends, has a large social network, crosses organizational boundaries, has an intrinsic desire to know, has an intrinsic drive to share knowledge, is hardly controllable by managers, has a lot of expert power.
Integrator	The champion participates in conversations with clients and customers, educates teams, considers the ecological footprints of the firm, contributes to the communal knowledge base for sustainable design and creation, initiates policies to ensure that sustainability becomes part of the mainstream operating values of the organization.

the champion who innovates. A more realistic assumption can be that a champion of innovation can be one of the key individuals of the innovation process; whether that champion is highly effective depends on cooperation with other champions, leaders, entrepreneurs and colleagues.

The research in this chapter indicates that championship for eco-innovation and sustainability can be a key function in the co-ideation process. The framework of characteristics of the champion of eco- and sustainable innovation is comprehensive (see Table 4.1). It shows an extensive range of possible behaviors, tendencies and traits. The framework indicates that the sustainable champion of innovation invests a lot of time and efforts in promoting new possible trajectories and business propositions. The champion knows how to stay informed and is at the center of various social networks in and around the firm. The sustainable champion of innovation integrates eco- and environmental issues into the backbone of the company and adopts some (maybe, but not necessarily, all) of the possible behaviors, tendencies and traits in this overview.

The research in this chapter indicates that these characteristics of sustainable champions can contribute to the development of sustainably innovative ideas, concepts, visions and initiatives in industry.

4.6 SUMMARY

Championship is the third element at the co-ideation level of the model of eco-innovation and sustainability management. The research shows that the sustainable innovation champion can perform various behavioral styles to stimulate the creation and diffusion of innovative ideas in the company. The champion of sustainable and eco-innovation knows how to promote new ideas and how to get others involved. Many people can be infected with the champion's ideas, stories and visions of what can or needs to be changed in and by the firm. The champion has a large network of contacts, which are situated in the firm and in the firm's environment. The champion uses these contacts to trace information, knowledge and the latest news and gets updates from various sources. The champion of eco- and sustainable innovation focuses on the development of ideas for sustainable products, services and business processes that work in practice. The champion of eco- and sustainable innovation is the third important individual type in the co-ideation process.

The co-ideation process is located in the sphere of the co-innovation process. At the co-innovation level, some of the ideas that originated at the co-ideation level become reality. The co-innovation level of the model of eco- and sustainable innovation is the subject of the next four chapters. The next chapter starts with the first element at this level, which is the innovation team.

5   Co-innovation in Teams

5.1   INTRODUCTION

The first category of organizational forms at the co-innovation level is the category of teams. In this category, small groups of leaders, entrepreneurs, champions of innovation and their colleagues transform the ideas that originate at the co-ideation level into practical business solutions. Eco-innovative and sustainable teams adopt the ideas from the eco-innovative and sustainable leaders, entrepreneurs and champions and put these at the center of attention. Effective innovation teams align their innovative work and outputs with the business processes of the firm and aim to improve the firm's profitability and effectiveness. The team realizes innovative goals that contribute to the existing qualities of the organization. It is not innovation per se that drives the team. The possibility of improving the company's competitive position, the opportunities to serve new groups of customers and the prospects of increasing market share are the main driving forces behind innovative teamwork. The innovation team continuously keeps its eyes and minds on the innovation goals it sets. It retains a constant focus on these goals by realizing new business proposals, not by redeveloping old and well-known business routines. The sustainable innovation team has these qualities and is very aware of the importance of real teamwork, of a consistent and continuous focus on cooperation among all team members, including those who come and go. Sustainably innovative teamwork is needed to transform the ideas that are generated by the key individuals at the co-ideation level into innovations in business. The eco- and sustainable innovation team is the first element at the co-innovation level of the model of eco-innovation and sustainability management (see Figure 5.1).

This chapter organizes theory that forms the basis of the eco-innovation and sustainable team element of the model (Section 5.2). It describes the methods used to further develop the analytical validity of this element for industry (Section 5.3) and continues with an exploration of the analytical value of this element in practice (Section 5.4) and in theory (Section 5.5). Finally, it concludes with a summary (Section 5.6).

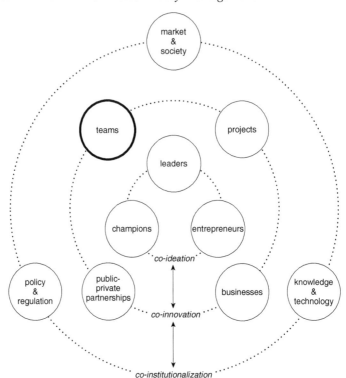

Figure 5.1   Co-innovation in teams.

5.2   THEORETICAL BASIS

An innovative team in a company is a dynamic organizational form. Teams can be formed by top management and put to work with an official assignment. In addition to this, professionals in firms can also form a team themselves, without instructions from their managers, and work on issues that they consider important. Most teams, either formal or informal, are joined by persons for a short or long period of time, and the comings and goings of members depend on social ties in the firm and on the need for certain knowledge, experience, approaches and representation. An eco- and sustainably innovative team is busy transforming the ideas that survived at the co-ideation level into workable solutions for the firm. The team knows that it has the assignment, duty or will to work on ideas and solutions that deliver gains in the short term and at the same time contribute to long-term sustainability.

Systems Thinking

On a theoretical level, the innovation team can be modeled as an open system that operates on the basis of exchanges with its business environment. This means that team members perceive their innovation team as an entity that has to function in the context of a larger whole. The innovation team is part of an organization, and the organization is part of a business environment. A team deals, for example, with suppliers and customers. In this context, the innovation team needs to find ways to innovate and has to concentrate on producing innovations that can be made by the organization the team is situated in, as well as sold to the markets the organization serves. The innovation team does not stand by itself and must be of service to its outside world. The search for innovation is not a search for innovation in itself but a search for renewal that strengthens the company, is of value to the customer and actually can be produced and marketed by the firm. A basic principle is that not the team but the organization and the business environment that surround the team determine the usefulness of innovations developed by the team. For an innovation team, it is important to regularly reflect on the wishes of the customer, the capabilities and abilities of the company and the company's suppliers' willingness to adapt to changing demands and wishes of the organization. The innovation team must be aware of the exchanges and transaction processes with its business environment and has to take into account that this has consequences for the teams' actions and performance (Björkman, 2004; Hülsheger, Anderson and Salgado, 2009).

Realistic Creativity

It can be difficult for innovative teams to be creative and realistic at the same time. A team that is creative and realistic at the same time encourages its members to work on creative options that instantaneously contribute to the company's goals and save or generate money. There are many management methods that enable people to generate and stimulate creativity and help people to overcome psychological barriers to being creative. For example, people might join a workshop and learn to think "outside the box." However, these methods often do not pay much attention to the costs associated with creativity and creative action. Neither do many of these methods address the revenues that have to come from a workforce with increased creativity. Combining a creative approach with realism goes one step beyond and is the essential concept of realistic creativity. When the members of a team have learned to create, for example because they have been successfully trained in brainstorming techniques or have been taught to envision the future, this does not mean that all creative ideas will be realized immediately. Often, creativity does not directly lead to new products and services that can be made and sold immediately. Teams with a realistic approach invest in idea generation, development and adoption but also select and focus on the innovative ideas with the highest potential market value. This puts a different light on the creative process. Ideas that seem very expensive or that do not open new markets can be dropped. Simply put, the options with the most market and sales potential survive (Kratzer, Leenders and Van

Engelen, 2006; Mathisen, Einarsen, Jørstad and Brønnick, 2004; Mathisen and Torsheim, 2006).

Innovation Focus

Teams may need a focus on innovation in words and deeds. Teams that focus on innovation emphasize that everyone in the team has to be innovative and oriented toward the team's innovative goals and spirit. This means that the team members' ambition is to develop an innovative culture and practice. Because team members are often located in departments in which the status quo and exploitation of "the old" are important, the creation of such a culture is not easy. Some examples of an innovative team spirit and practice are team members who take initiative and do not just wait for others to come up with something; team members who think about the possibilities of the plans of others instead of criticizing them; and team members who look at opportunities, who are less aware of risks and who prefer to learn by trial and error. These innovation-centered behaviors can be part of the unwritten rules, agreements, practices and social cohesion of the team. Team participants can be aware that they must put effort into improvement and innovation each day. They work on the basis of the concept that the final goal or the perfect situation may not exist and that business can always be done better or differently (Adarves-Yorno, Postmes and Haslam, 2007; Eisenbeiss, Van Knippenberg and Boerner, 2008).

Cooperative Drive

To be effective, an innovation team may need support from and cooperation with other members of the organization in which the team is situated. Teams with a cooperative drive concentrate on cooperation as a means to implement new processes, product designs and service procedures in their organization. Cooperation can tempt people in the organization to adopt the team's innovative proposals. Tight cooperation can increase the possibility that people will see an opportunity or challenge in innovative propositions that initially scared them. It is often argued that many people are resistant to change. Innovation is change. Innovation leads to new products and services that have to be produced, marketed and sold. Moreover, the organization does not exactly know how that works. For many innovative product concepts, for example, production processes and marketing campaigns are nonexistent. These have to be invented and created to produce the innovative product on a large scale. An innovative team thus may have to cooperate with people from business processes such as engineering, production, and marketing and sales to create a new organizational infrastructure that can turn the innovative ideas into business. Cooperation is needed to organize the production and commercialization process (Acha, Gann and Salter, 2005; Martinsuo, 2009). While cooperation is often a condition for innovation, it surely is a condition for sustainable innovation. Lejano and

Davos (1999) stress the importance of cooperation for sustainable innovation. An issue Lejano and Davis (1999) discuss is that cooperation comes at a cost, that people have to invest in it and that the gains are not automatically and fairly distributed among the cooperating actors. A fair distribution of revenues can be dealt with in a process of ongoing negotiation between the cooperating team members and their associates and forms an essential element of the cooperation process.

5.3   RESEARCH METHOD

Additional empirical and theoretical studies are performed to further increase the analytical value of the team element of the model of eco-innovation and sustainability management for industry.

Step 1.   Shaping the Research Model

This chapter builds on the results from the initial study of Bossink (2011a) (see Appendix 1). It focuses on the team element of the model (Section 5.2) and conducts empirical research in the Dutch metal industry to investigate how the team element of the model holds for another empirical context (Section 5.4). It then carries out a literature review on eco- and sustainable innovation teams in order to explore how the team element of the model can be shaped toward a broader analytical value for industry (Section 5.5).

Step 2.   Conducting Theoretical and Empirical Studies

Literature databases are consulted for research papers on teams and teamwork for environmental, ecological, green, social, societal, biological and sustainable innovation in business, firms and industry. In addition to this, ten managers and experts in the Dutch metal industry are interviewed and are asked to reflect on the sustainability issues they think are important for sustainable innovation (Van der Wiel, 2010).

Step 3.   Analyzing and Synthesizing the Studies' Outcomes

The team element in the initial model (Bossink, 2011a) is confronted with the empirical and theoretical studies. On the basis of the outcomes of this analysis, the characteristics of the team element at the co-innovation level are articulated for industry (Section 5.5).

5.4   EXPLORING THE EMPIRICAL FIELD

The interviews confirm that teams can have an influence on co-innovation processes for sustainability. Above all, the interviews point out that it is important that teams cooperate with other teams in their own organization and with teams from other organizations. It is teamwork that can improve the sustainability of supply and production chains that often intersect organizations and even industrial sectors. This section describes how teamwork can contribute to improved practices for material reuse, recycling and disposal. It is taken from Van der Wiel, Bossink and Masurel (2012, pp. 96–113).

Systems Thinking

Most respondents are aware of their relative position in the larger system of firms, authorities and institutions. They understand that sustainable improvements have to fit within a broader context. Six respondents, for example, recognize that regulatory force in the system is a significant driver of innovation by companies. With respect to this, an interviewee says: "Sustainability starts with regulation. Some time ago, nobody cared about the environment, and everybody could dump their waste on landfills, without too many restrictions. Nevertheless, when environmental problems increased, regulation became stricter." The respondents agree that regulation pushes them to do something. They feel obliged to respond, but they all struggle with the issue of how to improve practice while the bigger picture is diffuse, volatile and seemingly impossible to control. Companies try to keep up with the changes in the world around them and say that it is not just that they have to comply with regulation but also that they try to improve their sustainability scores for economic reasons. All interviewees, for example, are aware that raw materials may become increasingly scarce and expect that the costs of natural materials will increase. Nine respondents expect that team efforts that focus on increasing the reuse and recycling of materials can yield higher profits or lead to cost reductions. Three respondents have not yet found the right business model to make money through the improved use, reuse and handling of materials. They, for example, state that the costs of material reuse and recycling are still not balanced by the associated cost reductions. Four interviewees expect that this will change for the better in the coming years.

Realistic Creativity

The interviewees share the opinion that new practices for the reuse and recycling of metals should be financially feasible and provide direct financial benefits. Product design methodologies, for example, can offer a down-to-earth approach to improve the reuse and recycling of materials in the product design stage. (For more information on sustainable design methodology, see Appendix 6.) The interviewees' responses indicate that their companies can do more to improve the sustainability scores of their products in the design stage. They, for example, mention the concept of "design for homogeneity," which is a design concept that aims to limit the use of different kinds of materials in product design. They state that this concept has potential and can be used more frequently; nine interviewees say that their firm does not use this concept structurally. On the other hand, several respondents state that another concept for design, so-called design for disassembly, has the attention of their companies' designers. This means that the designers create products that can be decomposed into their basic elements at the end of the life cycle. The interviewees also mention the standardization of components as a design concept that receives growing attention from their companies' designers. When components are standardized throughout different products and models, it can be easier and more lucrative to reuse components in the next product. It can, for example, reduce purchasing costs.

Innovation Focus

According to the respondents, teamwork that aims to increase the reuse and recycling of materials can be forced by outside pressure. Force from the outside can motivate a company to invest in a more material-efficient production process. The respondents mention various reasons for organizations' teams to focus on material innovations. A majority of the respondents, for example, says that reuse and recycling become strategic to their companies. Five of them say that they want to protect market share. They feel that being active in reuse and recycling adds to their green image and gives them a strategic advantage over their competitors. A respondent, for example, mentions competitive pressure as the reason that his company strategically chose to reuse and recycle: "We are now going to use it more as a marketing and strategic issue." Another interviewee's firm heavily invests in the reuse and recycling of materials "because it fits within our corporate social responsibility policy. Because we want to move to a higher cradle-to-cradle certification level [that is, a measure of the extent to which a company reuses and recycles materials], it is important to realize an active recovery program. We have been engaged in corporate social responsibility for a long time, and it fits nicely." Most respondents come up with similar reasons. They reuse and recycle materials as an extra service to their environmentally aware customers and are driven by the corporate social responsibility policy of their firm, by the quality system their firm applies to ensure the quality of their processes and products or by their firm's system to create a healthy and safe working environment for employees.

Cooperative Drive

All interviewees are very clear about the importance of collaboration in the logistical process in their industry. A respondent, for example, says with respect to this that "it is very important to find collaboration and help each other." But just because it is important, it does not follow that it is easy. Sometimes, logistical innovations that contribute to the environment seem unorthodox and difficult to realize. An interviewee exemplifies this with a new logistical concept of firm cooperation that is not common practice in his industry but perhaps can become common practice in the future: "It is difficult to imagine that I tell my supplier: 'I'm buying this from you, and in about ten years you will get it back from me. Then you need to recycle it yourself.'" Overall, the responses of the interviewees indicate that the reuse and recycling of metals is an issue that depends on cooperation and teamwork at a between-firm level. Interdependence is a key concept in innovative practices for the reuse and recycling of materials. All respondents are currently undertaking recycling actions. Seven are or want to be actively involved in the recycling of their own products, and all respondents are currently recycling their waste or packaging materials. Three interviewees think that recent price developments on the world trade market will open new opportunities. Commercial enterprises will recycle products from the metal industry, such as zinc, steel and lead, in response to increased prices for raw, natural and virgin resources. In addition to collaborating with these firms, several respondents state that they also want to increase cooperation within their own firms and to develop and improve material reuse and recycling practices internally. Seven respondents, for example, state that their companies repair defective products; three of the respondents' companies are active in refurbishment; and three remanufacture their products by disassembling them and then reusing the components that are of sufficient quality.

5.5   DEEPENING THE THEORETICAL BASIS

The review of the literature indicates that the success of team efforts for sustainable innovation can highly depend on people's cooperation skills.

Margerum (1999), who studied successful environmental management practices of companies, defines environmental management as "a holistic approach, considering the entire system . . . that acknowledges interconnections in both the physical and human systems . . . is goal-oriented or focusing on end points . . . and strategic, which includes focusing analysis . . . [and] . . . planning toward implementing actions" (p. 152). Margerum (1999) contends that successful practice in the field of environmental management is based on early cooperation among coworkers and on protecting this cooperative practice.

First, with respect to developing cooperation among team members, according to Margerum (1999), individuals in teams who start new sustainable initiatives can be supported by local and national authorities with regulation and governmental policy. Margerum (1999) also states that the government can do more to facilitate, stimulate and support team-based eco- and sustainable innovation. It can establish governmental and other public institutes that provide support to people who seek to cooperate with others and who want to form a team. This support can take the form of allocating resources for communication and administration, for organizing and attending public meetings, for hiring facilitators or for gaining publicity. Although people often begin initiatives in their spare time and by taking advantage of the organization's slack resources, the development of their activities into something of considerable size needs extra investments. In addition to support from the authorities, the starting individuals and the emerging teams around them need other stakeholders to support them and cooperate with them. The stakeholders need to be willing to cooperate and to be formally involved, and they have to deliver substantive contributions. In addition to this, Margerum (1999) stresses that it is important for teams and their sustainable innovation practices to be supported by many stakeholders. This creates a social basis for the teams' sustainable output. The team thus must be willing to offer membership to any interested party. This prevents the sustainable, social or societal results of the activities of the team from being challenged. People who are left outside may complain that the team serves only the particular interests of the participants and not public interests. Margerum (1999) continues that it is important that the team builds a broad understanding and achieves consensus among team members and between the team and the stakeholders. This builds support and unanimity over the long run and avoids reintroduced discussions, requests for extra information and deferred meetings. The concept here is that consensus builds long-term trust and support for the team's outcomes. Margerum (1999) substantiates that skillful people should lead the efforts of a team. A skillful central coordinator should be the main person in the collaborative process, and such a coordinator may need a wide range of skills and capabilities, including communication and conflict resolution skills, experience with planning processes, an understanding of the technology to work with, group facilitation skills and project management and strategic planning. Margerum's (1999) approach fits with the meaning of the team element in the model of eco-innovation and sustainability management. It stresses that a sustainably innovative team has to deal with interactions and interdependencies with its environment. It also supposes that a focus on innovation is a basic and necessary quality of a team. Moreover, it builds on the concept of cooperation as an essential characteristic. Besides this, there is also a remarkable difference between Margerum's (1999) approach and the team element of the model. While Margerum (1999) contends that sustainable teamwork must have public value and for that reason should aim for a continuous dialogue with and consensus among public stakeholders, the approach in the model of eco-innovation and sustainability management is that sustainable teams can be realistically creative and focus on profitable environmental, social and societal innovation. The team approach in the model acknowledges that teams have to deal with tradeoffs between profitability for shareholders and firm owners and the satisfaction of several stakeholder groups.

Second, Margerum (1999) continues with the argument that innovation teams need to be protected once cooperation has been initiated. Protection consists of several critical aspects. Members of the team need to communicate in a clear and effective way. They have to communicate plainly with their team members and with the stakeholders outside the team. In addition, cooperation needs to be protected. Teams can use ground rules, basic principles and standard management tools that guide their cooperative activities. Examples of practical instruments are meeting structures, assignments of tasks and responsibilities, and formalized procedures for decision making. With respect to the decision-making procedures, Margerum (1999) concludes that these should be unambiguous to prevent conflicts between team members. Margerum (1999) continues that it is important that the team members are willing to work on and capable of achieving conflict resolution, for example by means of additional research, extensive discussion, careful deliberation or intervention by a capable third party. Moreover, collaboration does not have to be without conflicts, which sometimes can be very productive and may lead to positive outcomes if handled effectively. Finally, Margerum (1999) substantiates that the members of a team can act because of a sound understanding of the sustainability problems and issues they aim to solve. Conceptual sustainable innovations need to be situated and implemented in the real world, which is often a complex web of humans and technologies. It is thus important that the team knows how the web functions, what the parameters are, what causes failure and what can be done to avoid it.

All elements of Margerum's (1999) argument add a new concept to the team element of the model of eco-innovation and sustainability management. Margerum (1999) specifies how systems thinking, innovation focus and cooperative drive in a sustainably innovative team can be organized and controlled.

The research in this chapter indicates that teamwork for eco-innovation and sustainability can have a central function in the co-innovation process. The frame of reference shows a range of characteristics of eco- and sustainably innovative teams (see Table 5.1). This does not mean that an eco-team or a social innovation team must have all these characteristics. It means that a team can have several of these characteristics but not necessarily all. The frame of reference indicates that the team can have an ongoing and strong focus on innovation and pay attention to the transformation of ideas into innovations that contribute to the firm's profitability and competitive position. In addition to this, the sustainably innovative team members can have a tremendous drive to cooperate with one another, in their own departments, across the boundaries of departments and across the boundaries of the company.

The research in this chapter indicates that the characteristics of sustainable teams can contribute to the transformation of sustainably innovative ideas, concepts, visions and initiatives into profitable, sustainable innovations in industry.

Table 5.1   Frame of Reference for Eco-innovative and Sustainable Teams

Teams	Characteristics
Systems thinking	The team is coordinated as a part of a larger whole, deals with suppliers and customers, is dependent on institutions, has to deal with regulation, can be influenced by financial incentives, needs support from the authorities, needs members who understand the relationship of the team with its business environment.
Realistic creativity	The team innovates within financial constraints, supports creative idea generation, selects creative ideas with market potential, integrates sustainable improvement in the firm's product and service designs, needs skilled leadership and participants, knows how to implement innovative solutions in the real world, is controlled by and protected with a portfolio of management tools.
Innovation focus	The team concentrates on innovation, has an innovative team culture, concentrates on the possibilities for continuous innovation and improvement, perceives sustainability as a strategic issue, aims to ensure the sustainable quality of its processes and output.
Cooperative drive	The team cooperates where beneficial, balances allocation of costs and revenues for team members, cooperates because of a shared interest, cooperates because of public interests, cooperates across the boundaries of departments and organizations, is supported by stakeholders inside and outside the firm.

5.6   SUMMARY

The team is the first element at the co-innovation level of the model of eco-innovation and sustainability management. The research shows that the sustainably innovative team can have many salient characteristics. The team is aware of its function in its business environment and knows that it has to develop innovations that fit with this context. It needs a realistic view on sustainability and concentrates on developing eco- and sustainable innovations that are profitable to both the firm and society. The team's focus on innovation is consistent and unremitting. Above all, the team members know that they have to cooperate and that cooperation can be found across departmental and organizational boundaries. The eco- and sustainably innovative team is an important organizational form that can structure co-innovative activity. The second important organizational form at the co-innovation level is the eco- and sustainably innovative project. This is the subject of the next chapter.

6 Co-innovation in Projects

6.1 INTRODUCTION

The second category of organizational forms at the co-innovation level is the category of projects. This category represents the temporary organizational structures in which various teams cooperate and transform innovative ideas into innovations for business. Projects and project management for eco-innovation and sustainability deal with realizing some of the innovative ideas that originate at the co-ideation stage by, for example, developing blueprints, basic designs, initial plans or prototypes. Projects define a time frame in which the team must realize the envisioned innovations while meeting several deadlines and achieving intermediate results in order to guide the cooperating teams. A project sets concrete targets that direct the project participants' efforts and steer their activities. The targets are set in terms of concrete and measurable deliverables that the project participants have to create at a predefined moment in the time frame of the project. The results of the sustainably innovative projects have an environmental, social or societal impact, and this impact is used to attract customers. The products and services that the projects aim to develop must have sustainable value as well as financial value and must have the potential to generate value to the customer, the producer, and the public. Sustainably innovative projects are needed to transform the ideas that are generated by the key individuals at the co-ideation level into innovations for business. Eco-innovative and sustainable projects form the second element at the co-innovation level of the model of eco-innovation and sustainability management (see Figure 6.1).

This chapter first introduces theory that forms the basis of the sustainable project element of the model of eco-innovation and sustainability management (Section 6.2). It continues with a presentation of the methods that are used to explore the analytical validity of this element of the model for industry (Section 6.3) and then explores the analytical value of the element in practice (Section 6.4) and in theory (Section 6.5). The chapter concludes with a summary (Section 6.6).

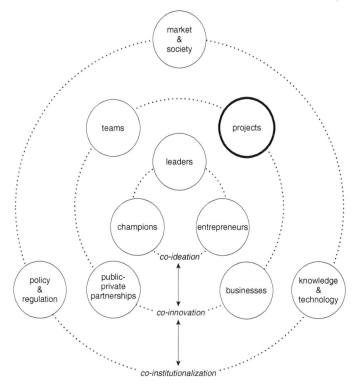

Figure 6.1 Co-innovation in projects.

6.2 THEORETICAL BASIS

In an innovation project, several teams cooperate to transform innovative ideas into innovations for the firm. A characteristic of an innovation project is its embedding in a company. Projects are often initiated by a company's management and frequently require that one or more teams cooperate to achieve a specific target or goal that is important to the company. A project has a time frame in which all activities are scheduled and are to be performed by the team members. Members' activities are coordinated by one or more project managers who see to it that the proposed results and outcomes are delivered. The innovation project is the domain of several professionals and teams. Often a dedicated project manager and several other permanent project members work for a project, advised, assisted and joined by many managers, coworkers, specialists and consultants who are temporarily associated with the project and who come and go during the project's time frame. An eco-innovative and sustainable project is mainly started to transform the sustainably innovative ideas that originated at the co-ideation level into tangible solutions, propositions, test cases and examples for the firm.

Results depend to a large degree on consistent planning in which all project activities are scheduled. The project leader, permanent members and temporary participants have to cooperate to deliver results and tangible outcomes. Project managers use targets to motivate and stimulate people to deliver results on time and within budget constraints. These intended results have to contribute to the firm's portfolio of products and services and have to increase the firm's opportunities to develop new markets.

Conception

At the start of a project, the key project participants, such as the project manager and the client (who often is a top manager in the firm), have to envision what they aim for. They need to have a certain plan of what they want to achieve, a conception of what the project has to be about and what it should deliver. They have to be aware that to a certain degree they can predetermine how the innovation process should go by the way they define the essential parameters, including the deliverables, milestones, targets and constraints of the project. The conceptualizing project manager tries to determine the course and outcomes of the innovation process before the project starts. The conception-oriented project manager thinks carefully about the time that is needed to complete the project and estimates the required budget. In addition, the project manager has a mental picture of the innovation results that should be achieved at the end of the project. Ideally, these thoughtful aspects of the project are put on paper. When the project plan is ready and approved by top management, it is ready to start (Dougherty, 2008; Kenny, 2003). The conceptualized project is based on a well-defined mental outline of how the project should go and this project plan is used to instruct the project participants (Dorenbosch, Van Engen and Verhagen, 2005). The project manager ensures that everyone knows what he or she is expected to do and does it. When, during the project, new and irresistible ideas arise, which is usually the case, the conception-oriented project manager does not allow these to wipe out the initial plan but chooses either to integrate the new ideas into the existing project plan or to put them aside (Shipton, West, Parkes, Dawson and Patterson, 2006). The project plan serves as an anchor, a blueprint and a clear directive for the project. It is a mental design of the route and outcomes of the innovation project.

Planning

Planning-oriented projects implement innovations systematically, stage by stage, milestone to milestone and iteration to iteration (Blindenbach-Driessen and Van den Ende, 2006). A planned project primarily focuses on achieving progress in time. At the start of the project, for example, the project manager proposes to schedule several meetings in a row, and all participants in the project are asked to reserve several dates in advance for this schedule of meetings. The meetings aim at coming to oral and written agreements on the innovations that need to be developed. In addition, the meetings are used to assess and ensure that the decisions, actions and promises the team members agree upon are protected and kept. When necessary, the planning-oriented project manager asks other top managers in the organization to exert pressure on their subordinates to contribute to the project and reminds people of their professional responsibility to get and stay involved (Aggeri and Segrestin, 2007). The planning-oriented project manager has to ensure that the innovation processes flow and that the desired outcomes become reality (Keegan and Turner, 2002; Killen, Hunt and Kleinschmidt, 2008). The planning-oriented project manager focuses on monitoring the agreements, on reminding the people who participate in the project of the agreements and expectations and on informing everybody about the project's progress and outcomes.

Targeting

Targeting in an innovation project means that the project members focus on defining innovation goals and on realizing these goals. Symbolic goals such as "becoming innovator number one in our markets" can go hand in hand with precise goal statements like "50 percent of our turnover has to be generated by products we did not have three years ago" (Plambeck and Taylor, 2007). The project manager, permanent members and temporary participants in the project define innovation goals that fit with the firm's strategic goals and concentrate on realizing them (Kenny, 2003). Target-oriented projects are characterized by continuous improvement of existing products, services and processes (Panizzolo, 1998). The project manager and project members' work is based on the concept that a goal can raise people's awareness and stimulate their creativity and that many people are determined to find a way to achieve a set target. They believe that when problems arise, people will come up with new and original solutions. It is also often assumed that targets can have a motivating effect on people, bind them and generate energy to work to an innovative end. A target can drive individual interests of people to the background in favor of that "bigger thing," that faraway dream that has to become reality. The targeting manager encourages people to think and act purposefully.

Positioning

A positioning-oriented innovation project uses innovation as a means to gain competitive advantage in the market. In a positioning-oriented project, product and service innovation is seen as an instrument to attract customers and to outperform competitors. The opinion of the manager with a positioning approach is that it is of great importance to develop new products and services that can be widely marketed and that contribute to the brand or image of the firm. In a positioning-oriented project, people look for innovations and changes that have detectable appeal to potential customer groups. Project leaders and members, for example, read customer satisfaction surveys, study and interpret the latest trends in society, keep informed of what the competition is doing and talk regularly with customers and stakeholders to develop a feel for the market (Beverland, 2005; Gann and Salter, 2000). Much time and energy are invested in informing customers about the innovations that the company develops through its innovation projects. The project participants listen to the questions raised by the potential customers and consider these while developing new products and services (Acha, Gann and Salter, 2005; Blindenbach-Driessen and Van den Ende, 2006).

Cost-Benefit Considerations

The project that is managed based on cost-benefit considerations is mainly trying to develop innovations that provide a maximum of revenues at relatively low cost. The innovations the project develops need to have the potential to gain a market share that will enable the firm to make a profit. In addition, the customer who buys the product must be fully convinced that the performance, design, aesthetics, functions and additional features of the products or services are worth their price. The cost-benefit-considering project is based on these principles and integrates economic, environmental and social sustainability. Sustainability can produce extra economic gains, for example through the efficient use and reuse of resources. In addition, the economic viability of new products or services can be improved by reducing their pollution profiles or environmental footprints and by reducing the costs of penalties and charges for unsustainable production and consumption. The sustainable, cost-benefit-oriented project considers the social and societal value of the innovations it develops and may aim to sell these for a premium price (Al-Saleh and Taleb, 2010).

6.3   RESEARCH METHOD

Additional empirical and theoretical studies are performed to further increase the analytical value of the project element of the model of eco-innovation and sustainability management for industry.

Step 1.   Shaping the Research Model

This chapter builds on the results from the initial study of Bossink (2011a) (see Appendix 1). It focuses on the project element of the model (Section 6.2) and conducts empirical research in the Dutch banking industry to investigate how the project element of the model holds for another empirical context (Section 6.4). It performs a literature review to explore how the project element of the model can be shaped toward a broader analytical value for industry (Section 6.5).

Step 2. Conducting Theoretical and Empirical Studies

Literature databases are consulted for research papers on projects and project management for environmental, ecological, green, social, societal, biological and sustainable innovation in business, firms and industry. In addition to this, thirteen managers and experts in or associated with Dutch banking are interviewed and asked to reflect on the sustainability issues they think are important for co-creating sustainable innovation (Verloop, 2008).

Step 3. Analyzing and Synthesizing the Studies' Outcomes

The project element in the initial model (Bossink, 2011a) is confronted with the additional empirical and theoretical studies. On the basis of the outcomes of this analysis, the characteristics of the project element at the co-innovation level are defined for industry (Section 6.5).

6.4 EXPLORING THE EMPIRICAL FIELD

The interviewees confirm that all forms of project management can contribute to eco-innovation and sustainability in business. The exploratory interviews indicate that, in innovation projects, the ideas that originate at the co-ideation level can be transformed into innovations with market potential. The innovation project develops and adopts planning schemes and targets to get near to the envisioned innovations and is useful in creating a competitive position for a firm's new sustainable activities. This section is the author's interpretation of Verloop (2008), and quotations are taken from that source.

Conception

Sustainability is seen as an important part of a bank's effort to develop an innovation strategy. A strategic approach of eco-innovation and sustainability often starts with the development of ideas about what the sustainability concept means to the company. Eco-innovation and sustainability can be made part of the firm's strategy and can become a guiding principle for the projects and activities of the firm. Two respondents in this respect say that one of the Dutch banks "has a very good policy regarding environmental sustainability. . . . They implement corporate social responsibility issues in their strategies" (p. 47). Nevertheless, having a strategy and integrating sustainability in a corporate strategy is maybe not enough. People may need more than a mission statement that contains the words "eco," "environment" and "sustainable future." The interviews indicate that people need to be consistently and constantly informed about the measures and actions of their company in this area of sustainability, and they also want to know how and to what degree this contributes to the performance of the firm. With respect to the necessity of informing employees about the concept of sustainability, one of the respondents says that "communication is a very important tool. Every multinational has a corporate sustainable responsibility report, but I think only a few employees will actually read this. This is the start: let all the employees read the corporate responsibility report. Then, departments have to organize a meeting occasionally, and in these meetings, the corporate sustainable responsibility report can be discussed. You have to address 'environmental sustainability' permanently. Furthermore, I would make environmental sustainability an evaluation criterion for the assessment of employees' performance" (p. 51). The interviews indicate that conception can be an essential aspect of eco-innovative projects and activities in banking.

Planning

Sustainability is more than a concept and a few words in a mission statement. It is an issue that needs to be made operational and has to be integrated in the firm's operations. A respondent working as a bank manager, for example, states that it is important "to translate an environmental policy to operational activities. Our managing director for sustainability is seen as an authority. People of his [central] department keep in close contact with [our local offices], and promote that they hire their own local coordinator for corporate social responsibility. Thus, corporate social responsibility is incorporated. I think that is good" (p. 49). Moreover, incorporation of sustainability in a firm often starts with innovative projects that teach the people what sustainability is and how it can be integrated in existing activities. An interviewee who works for a consultancy firm that supports companies to develop sustainable innovation projects refers to two examples of companies' attempts to plan sustainable activity: "[One of our clients, a multinational] set up a world-wide project . . . [and], . . . by means of this project, tries to increase their employees' consciousness of the environmental problems in the world. Another example of an organization that involves its employees is a large production company that asked for input of its employees for its environmental policy. The employees were consulted regularly by organizing a monthly meeting. . . . In this meeting they discussed the firm's current position regarding environmental sustainability, and which actions they had to take" (p. 51). The interviews show that a systematic planning of sustainable action in and by the firm can receive considerable attention.

Targeting

The interviews also indicate that many organizations do not know how to set and accomplish eco-innovative targets. They often are not sure of how to start or how to obtain resources to begin with a sustainability project. Many firms do not know how they should aim for sustainability and how they can receive financial support from a bank. An interviewee of a consultancy firm for sustainability and corporate social responsibility, for example, responds that "there are a lot of regulations to stimulate the introduction of sustainable innovations onto the market, but in my opinion, supply and demand is not geared towards each other. I recently talked to [a large Dutch bank] and they had budget to invest in sustainable initiatives . . . but nobody submits a request for this! That makes you wonder whether start-up enterprises know what the possibilities are" (p. 38). A similar remark is made by another respondent from one of the large Dutch banks, who recognizes that entrepreneurs and firms do not always know where to go to get funding for their first sustainable innovation project: "Starting enterprises that want to introduce a sustainable product or service to the market can go to a bank and obtain a loan. . . . An entrepreneur can also directly go the government, which offers loans or subsidies for these projects. I think this is not known by a lot of entrepreneurs" (p. 39).

Positioning

The interviews indicate that firms that decide to compete on the sustainability factor often try to go it alone. This conflicts with the generally accepted notion that eco-innovation and sustainability can benefit from cooperation. A respondent who works for the sustainability department of one of the big Dutch banks puts it as follows: "Sustainability can be an area of tension: on the one hand sustainability can lead to competitive advantage; we see increasing marketing on sustainability by firms nowadays. On the other hand, if you really want to accomplish something you need to work together" (p. 37). In addition, a respondent from a consultancy firm for eco-innovation and sustainability says about the practices of Dutch banks in general: "I think banks try to compete with each other in the area of corporate social responsibility and sustainability. This conflicts with a collaborative approach . . . in an ideal situation you work together to stimulate sustainability, because it enables you to accomplish more" (p. 37). The interviews indicate that it will take considerable time for firms to find a new balance between competition and collaboration.

Cost-Benefit Considerations

Firms still struggle with how to balance investments in sustainability with returns on these investments. It appears to be difficult to transform an organization and its processes, procedures and projects in favor of sustainability. Firms do not always know what to do and do not know when their business is judged to be sustainable. Customers struggle with the same issues. A respondent from a large Dutch bank for example states that "Consumers' decision to buy something is based on the price and quality of the product, and less on what the environmental consequences are. . . . You see environmentally sustainable products all the time, but you should wonder what such a product actually is. Take the 'sustainable credit card' as an example. What is it that makes this credit card sustainable? And a so-called 'climate-mortgage'? What is that? And what are the consequences of this mortgage? This needs to be explained to the consumers" (p. 41). Most of the respondents emphasize the importance of developing knowledge. A well-educated and informed workforce knows better how to integrate the sustainability aspect into the innovation processes and projects of the firm. A respondent who works for one of the large banks in the Netherlands says: "Last year we educated our employees. We taught them which corporate sustainability criteria they need to bear in mind if they decide to finance a company" (p. 53). The interviews draw an overall picture of banks that, step by step, explore and find ways to combine a business-for-profit with a business-for-profit-and-sustainability approach.

6.5   DEEPENING THE THEORETICAL BASIS

The review of the literature points out that projects can lack knowledge about the sustainability targets that can be set and the measures that can be used.

Labuschagne and Brent (2005, 2008) and Shen, Tam, Tam and Ji (2010) argue that to really be eco-innovative and sustainable, an innovation project needs to adopt sustainable performance indicators, in addition to the traditional indicators such as financial and organizational measures. Attributes that are important in a sustainably innovative project are the conditions of and the impact on air, water, land and resources and the conditions of, impact on and relationships to human resources, stakeholders and societal issues and groups. (For more about targets and measures, see Appendix 7.)

According to Labuschagne and Brent (2005) there is a large quantity of optional measures that can be used to assess a project's impact on air, water, land and natural resources. A project that aims to improve a firm's impact on air, water and land quality and to decrease the company's use of natural resources can, for example, measure and monitor its performance by assessing the performance indicators and measures listed in Table 6.1 (first row). The table indicates that global warming is one of the potentially hazardous effects of projects' and firms' activity. In addition to this, there are many other potential hazards that can be caused by projects and firms and that can be taken into account, including the acidification of the air, toxicity and

Table 6.1 Environmental Impact Indicators (based on Labuschagne and Brent, 2005, 2008)

Environment	Element	Environmental impact indicator	Measure
Ecological	Air	Acidification potential	kg sulfur dioxide (SO_2) equivalents
		Photochemical ozone-creation potential	kg ozone (O_3) equivalents
		Global-warming potential	kg carbon dioxide (CO_2) equivalents
		Stratospheric ozone-depletion potential	kg freon-11 (CFC-11) equivalents
	Water	Eutrophication potential	kg phosphate (PO_4) equivalents
		Human toxicity potential	kg lead (Pb) equivalents
		Eco-toxicity potential	kg lead (Pb) equivalents
	Land	Land occupation and transformation	m^2 degraded
		Human toxicity potential	kg lead (Pb) equivalents
	Resources	Mineral depletion	kg platinum (Pt) equivalents
		Energy depletion	kg carbon (C) equivalents
Soci(et)al	Human resources	Employment stability	# permanent jobs created
		Employment practices	average working hours
			ratio female to male workers
		Health and safety	% of budget spent on health and safety
			# health and safety accidents
	Social context	Personal development	% of budget spent on education and training
		Development of municipal area	% increase/decrease in housing prices
			% increase/decrease in educational level
	Societal context	Stakeholder participation	# stakeholder meetings
			# community forums
		Stakeholder influence	# channels for complaint and participation
		Socioeconomic performance	contribution to institutional environment, such as introduction of new standards and regulation contribution to regional gross domestic product (GDP)

Table 6.2   Frame of Reference for Eco-innovative and Sustainable Projects

Projects	Characteristics
Conception	The project envisions its course and outputs, predefines what it has to deliver, is based on a social contract between client and project leader, communicates to its participants what the innovative outcomes have to be.
Planning	The project is based on a time frame and planning, is coordinated, delivers results step by step, is managed through activity schedules, monitors agreements and progress.
Targeting	The project manages toward goals, uses incentives to reach goals, selects goals that fit with the firm's strategy, guides people's behavior, applies environmental, social and societal performance indicators and measures.
Positioning	The project contributes to the firm's competitive position, contributes to the firm's market appeal, adds to the firm's brand, is informed of customers' demands and trends, strengthens the firm's capability to compete on eco-innovation and sustainability.
Cost-benefit consideration	The project balances financial and sustainable goals, uses financial and sustainable-performance indicators and measures, has a system for the assessment of the environmental, social and societal quality of the products and services it produces, quantifies the sustainable outputs, attracts customers who appreciate these outputs, contributes to financial growth of the firm.

land degradation. The impact indicators and measures can support firms as they choose which measures and targets they will use to guide and evaluate their sustainable innovation projects.

Labuschagne and Brent (2005, 2008) also present several useful environmental-impact indicators for soci(et)al elements that can be used to assess a project's influence on its wider social and societal context. The environmental-impact indicators for the human, social and societal context are listed in Table 6.1 (second row), which shows that a project can both enrich and contribute to the development of the people who work on it and can harm them. The social and societal issues listed in Table 6.1 became part of the corporate agenda of incumbent firms several years ago, as topics like personal development, education of personnel, communication and dialogue with and participation of stakeholders, and safety and health care became strategic corporate issues.

The research in this chapter indicates that eco-innovative and sustainable projects can have a central function in the co-innovation process and provide a hands-on, target-driven, temporary organizational structure for teams working to develop innovations for the firm. The frame of reference in Table 6.2 lists the possible characteristics of an eco- and sustainable innovation project. The framework shows that a sustainable innovation project may need an eco-innovative vision and careful planning to ensure that sufficient progress can be made and that the project is completed within a certain time frame. In addition, targets can guide the innovative activity of the project participants. The sustainably innovative project has to provide financial revenues to the firm, as well as functional, physical and emotional benefits to the customer.

The research in this chapter indicates that the characteristics of sustainable projects can contribute to the transformation of sustainably innovative ideas, concepts, visions and initiatives into profitable, sustainable innovations in industry.

6.6 SUMMARY

The project is the second element at the co-innovation level of the model of eco-innovation and sustainability management. The research shows that the sustainably innovative project has several characteristic features. The project offers sustainable products, services and competencies to the firm, is planned carefully, works with concrete and measurable sustainability targets and knows how improvements and innovation in the field of sustainability can contribute to the firm's competitive position. On top of this, it develops innovations that appeal to a customer who is willing to pay extra for improved and enhanced quality. The eco- and sustainably innovative project is an important organizational form that structures co-innovative activity. The third important organizational form at the co-innovation level is the eco- and sustainably innovative business, which is the subject of the next chapter.

7   Co-innovation in Businesses

7.1 INTRODUCTION

The third category of organizational forms at the co-innovation level is the category of businesses. The sustainably innovative business stands for the commercial firm or several cooperating firms that transform the sustainable ideas that originated at the co-ideation level into innovations that can be sold to the customer. The sustainably innovative business differs from the traditional business in the sense that it delivers value that is sustainable; it integrates economic, ecological, biological, social and societal value. A sustainable business tries to find new ways to delight customer groups, and often an organization has to cooperate with other organizations to create and commercialize new business propositions. Selecting, finding and choosing partners to co-innovate with are essential elements of the innovation process and can take a lot of time. Once organizations agree on the joint business proposal to be developed, they may start a joint venture, alliance or other kind of cooperative organizational form. In these organizational structures, they can develop the desired innovations and exploit these in one or more market segments. The eco-innovative and sustainable business aims to preserve the environment and tries to add additional environmental, social and societal value. It seeks synergy and improvements by integrating and balancing the economic, environmental, social and societal specifications of the products and services it develops. Moreover, it wants to serve shareholders as well as all kinds of other stakeholders inside and outside the firm. The sustainably innovative business is highly aware that growing groups of customers may be willing to pay a price for sustainable quality and focuses on this. Sustainably innovative businesses are needed to transform the ideas that are generated by the key individuals at the co-ideation level into innovations. Eco- and sustainably innovative businesses are the third element at the co-innovation level of the model of eco-innovation and sustainability management (see Figure 7.1).

This chapter first organizes the theory that forms the basis of the sustainable business element of the model (Section 7.2). It then describes the methods used to explore the analytical validity of this element for industry

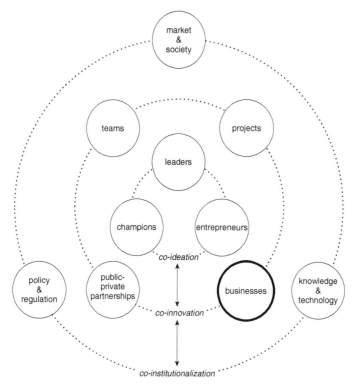

Figure 7.1 Co-innovation in businesses.

(Section 7.3), continues with an exploration of the analytical value of this element in practice (Section 7.4) and in theory (Section 7.5), and concludes with a summary (Section 7.6).

7.2 THEORETICAL BASIS

New businesses are often developed by several cooperating and co-innovating teams working on various projects and in one or more organizations. To conquer the market, the innovative ideas that originated at the co-ideation level can be realized in an organizational structure that enables mass production and mass marketing. A characteristic of a successful sustainably innovative business is that it is developed and exploited by a combination of cooperating commercial firms and public organizations. Often two or more organizations join forces to fight for new market share. They collaborate to transform the innovative ideas into business proposals, develop partnerships to combine and share one another's complementary competences and resources and establish joint ventures to produce and exploit the innovations on the marketplace. An eco-innovative and sustainable business wants to create extra value. It uses renewable resources, has clean production processes and owns aesthetic and ergonomic quality.

New Sustainable Business Development

Many organizations that develop new sustainable business consider the economic opportunities and risks of co-innovation with other companies (Fisher and Varga, 2002; George and Farris, 1999). On the one hand, these companies need technological and financial support from other sources to develop something new; on the other hand, cooperation with others also means that companies have to share knowledge, turnover and profits. At first sight, cooperation seems less beneficial than going it alone. While it can be beneficial to broaden the innovative firm's horizon and to share, combine and synergize other companies' complementary resources, it can cost considerable time and money to find the right partner. On top of this, when the right partner is found, it can be difficult to align firm cultures and business routines (Kreiner and Schulz, 1993). In the process of searching for one or more partners, the firm can be confronted with several questions. What does it specifically want to develop? What does it need from a partner? At what cost? And in what kind of cooperative structure? The literature indicates that it is difficult for firms to explicate these aspects of the co-innovative process. The literature also stresses that new business development is a process of making and keeping agreements between partnering organizations (Ring and Van de Ven, 1994). Partnering organizations have to deal with problems such as how to agree on each partner's input and exploitation of resources, how to jointly organize new product and service development, production and marketing, and how to distribute financial costs and benefits. This all means that firms that want to engage in new business development have to be able to deal with the pros and cons, gains and costs and difficulties and advantages of interfirm co-innovation. The co-innovative process can be complex and receives a lot of attention in the literature, which, for example, elaborates on the influence of regulation, markets and societal issues on firms' innovation practices (Bianchi, 1996). Other issues that are frequently addressed in the literature are the lengthy process of finding ways to cooperatively innovate (Bönte and Keilbach, 2005) and the negotiation processes partnering firms have to go through to ensure that they all invest in and benefit from the cooperation (Baraldi and Strömsten, 2009). Various research projects delve into the oral and written contracts that partnering firms use in the co-innovative process (Chiesa and Manzini, 1998), what partners can do to establish and govern a joint venture (Håkanson, 1993; Rampersad, Quester and Troshani, 2010), and how they organize production (Calia, Guerrini and Moura, 2007) and exploitation of their joint innovations (Calia, Guerrini and Moura, 2007).

The process of co-innovative new business development can be described as a trajectory of sequential activities (Fisher and Varga, 2002; George and

Farris, 1999; Kreiner and Schulz, 1993) that partnering organization can go through and start, interrupt and repeat all the time to organize their cooperative ambitions (Ring and Van de Ven, 1994). The linear trajectory of co-innovating firms can be described as follows. Firms that do not have the capabilities to innovate on their own try to explore the possibilities of co-innovation with others (Dell'Era and Verganti, 2009; Spithoven, Clarysse and Knockaert, 2010). Firms persistently and cautiously negotiate the resources, knowledge and capabilities each organization has to bring in (Baraldi and Strömsten, 2009; Nieto and Santamaría, 2007). They also spend a considerable amount of time on negotiating the possible distributions of costs and revenues (Christensen, Olesen and Kjær, 2005; Nieto and Santamaría, 2007). When organizations are still interested in cooperating, have not stopped the negotiations and decide to actually co-innovate, they enter into a contract. They reach agreements about the distribution of the costs and the revenues (Christensen, Olesen and Kjær, 2005; Vuola and Hameri, 2006). On the basis of these contracts and agreements, firms then develop innovation plans. In these plans, the organizations lay down which innovations they want to produce, how they will cooperate and what the individual and shared responsibilities are (Vuola and Hameri, 2006). Firms then establish an organization for co-innovation through which they are going to develop the innovations they planned (Rampersad, Quester and Troshani, 2010; Vuola and Hameri, 2006). This organization can have many forms; it may be an alliance, a joint venture, a learning network, or an R&D consortium (De Man and Duysters, 2005; Rampersad, Quester and Troshani, 2010; Thorgren, Wincent and Örtqvist, 2009). The cooperating organizations decide which governance structures they want to use to manage the joint organization (Rampersad, Quester and Troshani, 2010; Thorgren, Wincent and Örtqvist, 2009) and then start to realize the innovations. The co-innovating organizations use traditional management methods, such as project management and control systems, to plan and control the innovation processes (Calia, Guerrini and Moura, 2007). To sell the innovative products and services, the organizations intensively communicate with the market (Calia, Guerrini and Moura, 2007; Ritter and Gemünden, 2003) and position their innovations in one or more market segments (Ritter and Gemünden, 2003; Van de Vrande, De Jong, Vanhaverbeke and De Rochemont, 2009).

New Sustainable Business Exploitation

Once the innovations are realized and the business is developed, the co-operating organizations can focus on the exploitation of their innovative products and services. The sustainable products, services and business processes that originate from the new business development process constitute the firms' new business design. This new business design has several characteristics. Parrish (2010) introduces four sustainability requirements that need to be taken into account by organizations that wish to exploit their innovations. According to Parrish (2010), co-innovating organizations have to perpetuate resources, strategically satisfy a complex of criteria, stress the production of sustainable quality, and serve multiple stakeholders. A new business that perpetuates resources "produces benefit streams by enhancing and maintaining quality of human and natural resources for the longest possible time" (p. 517). Parrish (2010) continues that a sustainable new business design has to be embedded in its business environment, and the "foundational task of organizing is justifying the existence of an enterprise based on a common purpose" (p. 517). The new business also needs to stack benefits, strive for economic and sustainable goals and serve multiple stakeholders in the firm and in society. This "can be achieved by reaching a certain threshold, rather than the constant striving for maximization of one single, prioritized outcome . . . [and the] . . . structuring of enterprises so that as many beneficial outcomes for as many different stakeholders as possible" are realized (pp. 517–518). Parrish (2010) contends that to realize these goals, new business exploitation must be focused on creating and realizing quality, specifically sustainable quality. The firms in a new sustainable business organize their new product and service development activities around creating extra environmental, social and societal quality. The criteria for decision making in new sustainable businesses are particularly concerned with producing and offering better products and services and are based "on a logic of outcome quality rather than quantity" (p. 519).

7.3   RESEARCH METHOD

Additional empirical and theoretical studies are performed to further increase the analytical value of the business element of the model of eco-innovation and sustainability management for industry.

Step 1.   Shaping the Research Model

This chapter builds on the results from the initial study of Bossink (2011a) (see Appendix 1). It focuses on the business element of the model (Section 7.2) and conducts empirical research in various Dutch industries to investigate how the business element of the model holds for other empirical contexts (Section 7.4). It carries out a literature review of eco-innovative and sustainable business in order to explore how this element of the model can be shaped toward a broader analytical value for industry (Section 7.5).

Step 2.   Conducting Theoretical and Empirical Studies

Literature databases are consulted for research papers on firms and businesses for environmental, ecological, green, social, societal, biological and sustainable innovation. In addition to this, ten managers and experts in various industries in the Netherlands are interviewed and asked to reflect on the sustainability issues they think are of importance for sustainably innovative business (Mahawat Khan, 2010).

Step 3. Analyzing and Synthesizing the Studies' Outcomes

The business element in the initial model (Bossink, 2011a) is confronted with the additional empirical and theoretical studies. On the basis of the outcomes of this analysis, the characteristics of the business element at the co-innovation level are articulated for industry (Section 7.5).

7.4 EXPLORING THE EMPIRICAL FIELD

The picture that arises from the interviews is a picture of public organizations and commercial companies that try to develop new sustainable businesses in a business landscape that still is not used to sustainable initiatives. This section is the author's interpretation of Mahawat Khan (2010), and quotations are taken from that source.

New Sustainable Business Development

Several respondents stress the necessity of regulation as a means to force firms to start developing new sustainably innovative business. One of their typical arguments is that as long as there is no pressure, there is no incentive to change. Once there is pressure, for example from new regulation, firms start to feel and calculate the risks and advantages of (non)compliance. Risk avoidance and opportunity-seeking behavior then can move them in a more sustainable direction. As one of the respondents puts it boldly: "You have to sting and stab actors before they start to fight courageously and fearlessly" (p. 35). All respondents recognize that interaction with other organizations can be of benefit to their own organization. Because of this, it would be logical for the respondents' firms to engage in collaborations with other firms. Nevertheless, this is not always the case. The respondents say that there is a serious reason for not to be too open. This reason is either inadequate or total lack of trust. Several respondents state that they do not collaborate and that it is difficult to start a co-innovation process with another firm or organization. It can be a valuable undertaking but also a dangerous one. The question always is: Who can be trusted in terms of appropriation of knowledge and power, and who cannot? And another question is: How will the counterparts behave in the future, with the knowledge and experience they gained from their partners? Firms that want to engage in a co-innovative process have to make a judgment about the opportunities and risks of collaboration and must weigh aspects of collaboration such as knowledge leakage and changing distributions of power. This is articulated by one of the interviewees in a short and clear statement: "It is really simple, knowledge is power, and power is not something you want to share" (p. 32). However, not all respondents agree with this. They criticize this way of looking at competition and competitive dynamics and doubt this view's adequacy. With respect to this, a respondent states that "thinking in terms of competition is old thinking. In this networked and digitized economy you can have a leading role for just two months, after this period the whole world knows what you are doing, and how you are doing it" (p. 35). Both points of view exist at the same time, and most interviewees are aware of the tension between trusting partners and sharing information and knowledge on the one hand and being competitive and protecting the key resources of the firm on the other. Respondents indicate that they constantly explore what kind of organizational structures and procedures they can use to organize cooperative innovation that is based on trust and openness but that is also restricted by suspicion and secrecy. The firms of some of the interviewees, for example, experiment with setting up facilities and meeting rooms for their workers. These facilities enable people to interact with representatives from other companies and to informally explore the collaborative opportunities long before their firms' top managers decide to exchange crucial and competition-sensitive information. One of the interviewees is very enthusiastic about this new organizational feature and states: "I think we developed the way to cope with problems related to trust and competition" (p. 34). Some of the respondents go a few steps further. They advocate the concept of geographic areas with high concentrations of firms with complementary financial resources, knowledge, capabilities and ambitions, such as Silicon Valley in the United States. Silicon Valley has a high concentration of high-tech startup firms and is considered by many to be one of the most important areas for innovation development and exploitation. Some interviewees stress the importance of similar breeding places for innovation. To quote one of the proponents of geographic clustering: "Silicon Valley is the most telling example of significant innovation. We need something like that" (p. 33).

New Sustainable Business Exploitation

Respondents acknowledge that although the environmental issue receives growing attention, it is still not completely legitimate for their firms to invest all financial resources, knowledge and people in eco-innovation and sustainability. Firms still doubt whether customers want to pay extra for sustainable products and struggle with the question of how sustainable quality can best be sold to the customer. One of the respondents in this respect remarks that markets for sustainable products are sometimes not fully formed or nonexistent: "Before demand can be influenced, it is important that the sustainable energy solution can be labeled as legitimate. Without legitimacy a market will not arise" (p. 49). Most respondents stress that their firms still study and experiment with ways to combine financial profitability with sustainable production and exploitation models. In addition to that, firms struggle with the issue of how to build business propositions that integrate traditional financial objectives with new sustainable measures and how to satisfy all stakeholders at the same time. Some of the interviewees, for example, state that it is impossible to serve all stakeholders. One of them even summarizes this into advice for the Dutch nation: "In the Netherlands we have the habit to discuss everything with involved actors, and to listen to them regardless of the consequences. This needs to stop now" (p. 38). Moreover, another respondent states that "agreement is fine, but for some decisions you have to be aware of the fact that you cannot expect support from some actors" (p. 40). In general, the interviewees indicate that the specifications of their firms' eco-innovative and sustainable business designs are "under construction." The future success of the business designs will depend on the firms' ethical decisions and how they handle trade-offs between financial and sustainable profits. Some respondents argue that products and services with environmental quality can lure customers from unsustainable substitutes because natural resources will become scarce and customers will increasingly appreciate clean solutions and environmental, social and societal quality.

7.5 DEEPENING THE THEORETICAL BASIS

The literature review indicates that "resources" can be seen as one of the main elements on which firms can build their competitive position, viability and perspectives.

Starik and Rands (1995) and Shrivastava (1995) contend that society needs ecologically sustainable organizations. The sustainable firm minimizes its environmental impact per unit of production and invests in creating environmental, social and societal value. An ecologically sustainable industry forms a counterweight against overpopulation, overconsumption and the depletion and waste of resources. In a similar line of reasoning, Hart (1995) coins the "natural resource-based view of the firm." Hart (1995) builds upon insights that are developed by business strategy researchers, who contend that resources are the basic source of a firm's competitive advantage in business. Resource-based theorists see firms as "bundles of resources" (Rumelt, 1984), comprising all tangible assets (e.g., land, factories and equipment), intangible assets (e.g., patents, brands and technical knowledge), and organizational processes (e.g., product development, internationalization and marketing) from which managers can develop value-creating strategies (Bingham and Eisenhardt, 2008). Taking the firm as the unit of analysis, this theoretical stream argues that firms in a particular industry tend to be heterogeneous with respect to the strategic resources that they own or control and that these resources may not be perfectly mobile across firms. Consequently, resource heterogeneity between firms may be long lasting (Barney, 1991), and resources can become the basic means by which firms distinguish themselves from one another. In line with this, Hart (1995) argues that firms' "bundles of resources" also consist of their competences to reduce their environmental impacts and contribute to environmental quality. According to Hart (1995), sustainably competitive firms adopt three natural resource–based tactics to build their strategies: pollution prevention, product stewardship and sustainable development. Pollution prevention is the reduction of emissions and waste. Product stewardship is the reduction of the environmental burden imposed by the firm's products and services throughout their life cycle. Sustainable development is all the firm does to become a clean producer, making a social and societal contribution to stakeholders in industrialized and developing countries. Hart (1995) envisions future business landscapes in which firms minimize emissions, effluents and waste and, by doing this, have lower costs and increasing market shares. Eventually, firms with sustainable business propositions and designs will have an advantage over competitors that stick to old, unsustainable strategies. With natural resources becoming scarce and more expensive and with a growing world population, it is imaginable that this vision is closer to reality than ever. With respect to this, Fowler and Hope (2007) contend that companies that seek to incorporate sustainable business practices into their strategies perceive sustainability "as a continual process of organizational innovation and development on all fronts, rather than a sequential process that begins with pollution control . . . even companies at the forefront of sustainability have a lot more to do in order to reach the elusive goal of sustainable development" (p. 36). The natural resource–based view of the firm proposes that a sustainability strategy can become a key strategy for outperforming competitors and that obtaining a nature-based competitive advantage is a challenge that deserves a firm's attention and investments. Although the creation of a natural resource–based strategy is a complex and difficult task that takes time and effort, it may be that once a company achieves an edge over its competitors, it becomes relatively difficult for other firms to copy this strategic competence. This would explain why some firms have already started to experiment with sustainable business.

The research in this chapter indicates that eco-innovative and sustainable businesses have a central position in the process of environmental and sustainable co-innovation. New business development and exploitation are the two key organizational concepts in eco-innovative business creation. The frame of reference in Table 7.1 shows the key characteristics of eco-innovative and sustainable businesses. The essential message is that firms have to be active in eco- and sustainably innovative business development activities such as knowledge and information exchange, negotiations, formal and informal contracting and joint-venture formation. In addition to that, firms can develop the ability to exploit business models that generate

Table 7.1 Frame of Reference for Eco-innovative and Sustainable Businesses

Businesses	Characteristics
New sustainable business development	New business is developed with partners, is based on partners' complementary resources, depends on the outcomes of negotiations between the partners, is formalized by means of oral agreements and written contracts between partners, thrives on a certain degree of (dis)trust between partners, is produced by joint ventures.
New sustainable business exploitation	New businesses are designed to perpetuate resources, serve multiple stakeholders, realize both economic and sustainable goals, produce sustainable value and quality, keep up with societal developments, create a competitive advantage by means of pollution prevention, product stewardship and sustainable development, are exploited by joint ventures.

extra environmental, social and societal value, serve multiple stakeholders, are economically and sustainably viable and are based on a natural resource–based strategy.

The research in this chapter indicates that the characteristics of sustainable businesses can contribute to the transformation of sustainably innovative ideas, concepts, visions and initiatives into profitable, sustainable innovations in industry.

7.6 SUMMARY

Business is the third element at the co-innovation level of the model of eco-innovation and sustainability management. The research shows that sustainably innovative business has two characteristic aspects: new sustainable business development and new sustainable business exploitation. New sustainable business development comprises the efforts to organize the process of co-innovation between partnering firms and addresses the activities that are needed to exploit a sustainably innovative joint venture. In addition to this, new sustainable business exploitation includes the activities that generate a financial and sustainable profit from the sustainable business. It aims to perpetuate resources, create extra sustainable quality to the customer, serve multiple stakeholders and implement a natural resource–based strategy that consists of pollution prevention, product stewardship and sustainable development. The eco- and sustainably innovative business is an important organizational form that structures co-innovative activity. The fourth and final important organizational form at the co-innovation level is the public private partnership. This is the subject of the next chapter.

8 Co-innovation in Public-Private Partnerships

8.1 INTRODUCTION

The fourth category of organizational forms at the co-innovation level is the category of public-private partnerships. This organizational form enables commercial firms and governmental and nongovernmental organizations to co-innovate and work on substantive new practices. The distinctive characteristic of a sustainably innovative public-private partnership is its primary focus on creating a new practice that has ecological, social and societal quality. It searches for new ways to create a new sustainable modus operandi—or, to be more precise, modus co-operandi—for industry. The public-private partnership is an organizational form that is used to experiment and demonstrate and thus to show how the new sustainably innovative practice of the future can look. Firms and nongovernmental and governmental organizations that join these public-private partnerships become the leading innovators of industry and are often supported by national policy, funding programs and regulation. Organizations that do not join the sustainable public-private partnerships still have the opportunity to learn from them, look at them, study them and copy aspects and elements of them. The eco-innovative and sustainable public-private partnership is a multipartner public-private alliance that aims to develop practice that shows industry how and in what direction to innovate. The knowledge-intensive development of a new sustainable practice with a nationwide potential requires all participants to build a shared vision on sustainability. Participants also have to work on new cooperative ways to realize the new sustainable concept in practice. Sustainably innovative public-private partnerships are needed to transform the ideas that are generated by the key individuals at the co-ideation level into innovations for industry. Eco- and sustainably innovative public-private partnerships are the fourth element at the co-innovation level of the model of eco-innovation and sustainability management (see Figure 8.1).

This chapter presents theory that forms the basis of the public-private partnership element of the model (Section 8.2). It describes the methods used to explore the analytical validity of this element for industry (Section 8.3), and it continues with an exploration of the analytical value of this

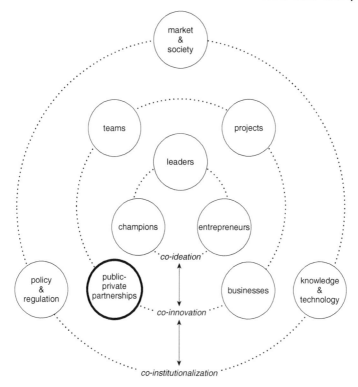

Figure 8.1   Co-innovation in public-private partnerships.

element in practice (Section 8.4) and in theory (Section 8.5). It concludes with a summary (Section 8.6).

8.2   THEORETICAL BASIS

A public-private partnership is often used when a nation wants to create an industry-wide breakthrough innovation program. To develop a program, several representatives, mainly heavyweight managers and directors of governmental, nongovernmental and commercial organizations, join force. These representatives deliberate on the actions to plan and the measures to take to implement a nationwide innovation program. All actors know that they have to invest in the plans and that they have to commit themselves. They all join the initiative because of the possible outcomes of the public-private partnership, which can be promising and worthwhile to invest in. Often, at the start, the governmental organizations have a national policy plan that is used as a guide for the development of the new co-innovative practice. Most developed countries have a scheme of regulations and subsidies to provide incentives to commercial actors to cooperate in public-private partnerships. In addition to this, the nongovernmental and commercial organizations bring in their own strategies, which vary from protecting the earth to developing sustainable and profitable businesses. An eco-innovative and sustainable public-private partnership heavily depends on the knowledge of the participating organizations. It needs all participants to be aware that the goal of their partnership is to create a new standard that can become the industry's next practice.

Governmental Push

The government can be seen as a major force behind the formation of public-private partnerships. It can use policy plans, regulation and economic incentives to create an atmosphere in which nongovernmental and commercial organizations are willing to join a public-private partnership and to develop new sustainable practices for industry.

Governments can develop national environmental policy plans to define the nation's sustainability goals for several years. The national environmental policy plans have consequences for the future direction of both public and private organizations and can be drivers behind the formation of sustainable public-private partnerships. In the national plans, for example, a government can state what the central, provincial and municipal authorities have to achieve in the field of sustainability. It can also state what is expected from commercial firms in industry (Kivimaa and Mickwitz, 2006). Many nations' environmental policies are based on the reports of the World Commission on Environment and Development of the United Nations (WCED). These policies define visions and action plans to work on sustainable development, which, according to WCED, means that "humanity has the ability to make development sustainable to ensure that it meets the needs of the present without compromising the ability of future generations to meet their own needs" (Brundtland and Khalid, 1987).

Regulation can be another key element of a governmental portfolio to stimulate eco-innovation and sustainability. Regulation can provide incentives that direct and stimulate innovative activity in sustainable public-private partnerships. The government also has the legal right to impose restrictions on governmental and commercial organizations. The basic concept is that the government is permitted to establish codes of conduct and levels of performance and that the authorities and private organizations have to work within the boundaries of these rules (Brío and Junquera, 2003; Nameroff, Garant and Albert, 2004). Many countries have general laws that can be used to set new or additional environmental requirements. Various countries, for example, already have laws on air pollution, noise, soil protection and waste management. By tightening the requirements of these laws, countries can quickly and effectively ensure some environmental limits.

Governments can also use financial incentives and obstacles to trigger industry to innovate in a sustainable direction. Subsidies and funding can stimulate companies to participate in environmentally friendly public-private partnerships. Peltier and Ashford (1998) argue that alternatives that are explored in a public-private demonstration can be attractive because they offer firms extra technical and financial assistance. The authorities can change the financial parameters to reorient firms' practices. An example of a financial incentive is a subsidy for energy-efficient cars, and an example of a financial obstacle is a governmental decision to increase dumping costs for unsorted waste. Both changes can lead to changed cost calculations for commercial actors (Kassinis and Vafeas, 2006).

Agreements

Governmental, nongovernmental and commercial organizations can use written and oral agreements to secure a certain level of sustainability in their work. In these agreements, governments, for example, can guarantee a part of the turnover of a sustainably innovative entrant in the industry. Or firms can (in)formally agree to dump waste in sorted fractions when the government reduces the dumping fees (Clark and Paolucci, 2001). A nongovernmental organization and a commercial firm can cooperate on sustainable issues and, for example, agree that the firm will decrease its ecological footprint in exchange for an official environmental quality endorsement from the nongovernmental organization. Or the government can negotiate covenants and codes of conduct with nongovernmental organizations and commercial companies. Although there is often no legal basis for such agreements and they cannot be used to force the parties involved to uphold their side of the deal, it is plausible that signatories will feel a professional and moral obligation to behave in a sustainably innovative way.

Next-Practice Creation

The public-private partnership can develop, create and demonstrate a "next practice" for industry. The innovative potential of a public-private partnership that consists of governmental organizations, nongovernmental organizations, universities, research institutes and knowledge-intensive firms can be immense. The exchange of knowledge among these actors can facilitate the development of new knowledge and industry's next practice (Goverse, Hekkert, Groenewegen, Worrell and Smits, 2001). To produce the building blocks for industry's next practice, the public-private partnership can be organized as an R&D consortium. In the R&D consortium, radical innovations in the field of sustainability can be invented, developed, tested and improved. Commerce, universities and scientific research centers and nongovernmental and governmental organizations can be the stakeholders of this consortium, and an important function of the public-private consortium for sustainable innovation can be its demonstrative effect. It shows to others what sustainable technologies and co-innovation routines can be used in regular projects in the country (Reijnders and Huijbregts, 2000; Sha, Deng and Cui, 2000). Usually the government subsidizes a public-private demonstration project, but this does not mean that it donates excessive financial resources to the commercial participants of the demonstration. In many cases, the commercial firms are asked to invest an equal amount in the project in the form of man-hours, the input of advanced knowledge and the participation of their top managers.

Although public-private demonstrations can have a knowledge-generating function, the knowledge from a demonstration does not flow to other organizations in industry by itself. Research by Harborne and Hendry (2009) and by Hendry, Harborne and Brown (2010), for example, points out that new eco-knowledge that is developed in a demonstration tends to flow exclusively to its participating firms and their future projects, not to the industry's traditional firms and their standard projects. Next-practice development by public-private partnerships seems to be particularly useful for the development of new knowledge and for demonstrating a possible next practice. The output of the demonstration can be seen as an assembly of knowledge that is tangible and accessible but that does not flow to industry spontaneously. Outside firms that want to appropriate this knowledge may have to actively study and learn from the demonstrations.

8.3   RESEARCH METHOD

Additional empirical and theoretical studies are performed to further increase the analytical value of the public-private partnership element of the model of eco-innovation and sustainability management for industry.

Step 1.   Shaping the Research Model

This chapter builds on the results from the initial study of Bossink (2011a) (see Appendix 1). It focuses on the public-private partnership element of the model (Section 8.2) and conducts empirical research in the Dutch food industry to investigate how the public-private partnership element of the model holds for another empirical context (Section 8.4). It carries out a literature review of eco-innovative and sustainable public-private partnering in order to explore how this element of the model can be shaped toward a broader analytical value for industry (Section 8.5).

Step 2.   Conducting Theoretical and Empirical Studies

Literature databases are consulted for research papers on environmental, ecological, green, social, societal, biological and sustainably innovative public-private partnerships. In addition, ten managers and experts in the Dutch food industry are interviewed and asked to reflect on the sustainability issues they think are important for sustainably innovative public-private partnerships (De Bruijn, 2009).

Step 3. Analyzing and Synthesizing the Studies' Outcomes

The public-private partnership element in the initial model (Bossink, 2011a) is confronted with the additional empirical and theoretical studies. On the basis of the outcomes of this analysis, the characteristics of the public-private partnership element at the co-innovation level are articulated for industry (Section 8.5).

8.4 EXPLORING THE EMPIRICAL FIELD

The exploratory interviews indicate that public-private partnering with the aim to create the next practice for sustainability is a complex matter that requires a lot of deliberation, mutual adjustment, investments and mental and social energy from partners. The interviews also indicate that the public-private partnership can be a powerful organizational form for the transformation of the ideas that originate at the co-ideation level into the next sustainably innovative practice for industry. This section is the author's interpretation of De Bruijn (2009), and quotations are taken from that source.

Governmental Push

Public-private partnering is complex, and its complexity starts with the nation's environmental policy planning process. The national environmental planning process is dependent upon the political situation in the country, which can be unstable. In the Netherlands, for example, the nation's population chooses the parliament every four years. In the Dutch democratic system, it never occurs that one single political party has more than 50 percent of the votes. Thus, political parties have to enter into a coalition with one or more other parties to be able to govern the country. Because governing coalitions regularly fall apart, elections often take place before the four-year period has ended. This shortens the time horizon of a governmental sustainability policy plan to four years or even less. In the words of a respondent, this hinders long-term governmental vision development: "The world is a complex place. When you solve one problem, it could be causing another problem somewhere else. That complexity is hard to . . . [address by] . . . the government, since they want to proceed to solutions too fast" (p. 50). The time frame of governmental policy seems to be shorter than the sustainability issue requires.

On a worldwide level, regulation is often characterized by disharmony. Regulation tends to differ from country to country. This makes it difficult for multinational firms to act in accordance with one specific and generally accepted law or code of conduct. Self-regulation is even more difficult. The sustainability issue is made of many subissues, consists of many parameters and can be interpreted in different ways (for more about sustainability issues and parameters, see Appendix 7). It impedes the development of quick and hands-on regulation that simply tells firms how to be sustainable. Respondents put forward that this is a serious problem in industry. One of the interviewees, for example, states that consumers start asking for more sustainability, but companies do not always know how to deal with this demand: "Awareness of consumers is increased by more information about production processes. . . . Certification [of production processes] results in more available information on products, which gives consumers the possibility to choose" (p. 51). The respondents' opinion is that worldwide regulation and codes of conduct can support companies to serve the environmentally conscious consumer.

The respondents frequently state that the economic climate is changing in favor of eco-innovation and sustainability. Sustainability is becoming a quality aspect that can be used by firms to create a competitive advantage. A respondent, for example, says that "sustainability can be used as a competitive advantage, since consumers seem to focus on it nowadays. Everybody knows that we should take care of our planet" (p. 42). The same respondent foresees a competitive race on sustainable quality in the near future in which "frontrunners are followed by others, which makes it even a bigger challenge for the front running firms to keep ahead of competition" (p. 42). Some of the interviewees envision an economic playing field that prioritizes sustainability, with consumers who are even willing to pay extra for more sustainable quality. A respondent emphasizes this by saying that "now sustainability is a societal issue, it is easier to make decisions in favor of sustainability, even when it increases costs" (p. 41).

Agreements

The respondents confirm that policy plans, regulation and economic incentives can be complemented by agreements between the partnering organizations in public-private partnerships. There are ample possibilities for agreement on codes of conduct internally as well as with partners. Tools that can be used are corporate responsibility reports (for more about the possible elements of such a report, see Appendix 7), industrial guidelines, product certificates (for more about sustainable product certificates, see Appendix 4), production agreements and environmental quality systems (for more about environmental quality systems, see Appendices 2 and 3). The respondents think that the public-private partnership is a sound organizational structure through which to collaborate, learn and improve sustainable standards and practices. Nongovernmental organizations often have a lot of knowledge of environmental and sustainable affairs and can be asked for help. A respondent perceives this as an opportunity to innovate: "The non-governmental organizations will support firms publicly, and want action from them in return" (p. 49). It stimulates the development of the nation's next sustainable practice.

Next-Practice Creation

Respondents see many opportunities for public-private partnerships to develop the next sustainable practice. An interviewee, for example, responds that "guidelines for suppliers, renewed mechanisms to deal with suppliers, and new performance measures" (p. 43) can be developed and improved by public-private initiatives. Respondents agree that production can be seen as a chain of activities that often transcends the boundaries of organizations and countries, with sustainable "innovation being crucial to the whole chain, starting at agriculture. All processes need innovation for sustainability, including the way we do business with suppliers" (p. 43). This broader scope could be a main pillar of next sustainable practice. Next sustainable practice does not concentrate on just one firm or business but involves others in doing business, as stated by one of the interviewees: "One should be aware of what stakeholders think. We are trying to map the stakeholders: who are our stakeholders and what do they think?" (p. 45). Respondents agree that where firms and other types of organizations connect, symbiotic relationships will sprout. One of the interviewees, for example, states that commercial firms today learn a lot from nongovernmental organizations: "Non-governmental organizations share their opinion, and strikingly they . . . take the costs for companies into account. They offer practical solutions. They are able to translate complex guidelines from the European Union to the company. They come up with very reasonable things" (p. 46). These "very reasonable things" touch upon people's and organizations' need for concrete actions and measures. Or, as one of the interviewees put it clearly: "Sustainability is the name of the journey, not of the final destination. Since this sounds very soft you should make it concrete" (p. 40). Making it explicit and concrete still leaves partnering organizations with difficult issues and problems to solve. Other respondents express it like this: "Sustainability should be a custom made concept since each situation is different" (p. 40), and "sustainability is a complex issue. It is hard to define shared goals; how far reaching . . . [our organization] . . . wants to be; how things should be formulated" (p. 40). They stress their own and their partners' responsibility to cooperate, deliberate and muddle through as long as needed to find ways to create the next sustainable practice. Mutual trust among the cooperating governmental, nongovernmental and commercial partners is crucial in finding solutions and creating new sustainable production and consumption patterns. One respondent expresses the importance of this process of continuous trial and error by stating that "it should be a real commitment. . . . The agreements should be very clear and that is why this starts with a behavioral code: how do we treat each other and what goals do we want to achieve? This has to be as concrete as possible, only then there will be commitment. It should not be just talking, it must be more than just knowledge sharing" (p. 54). The interviews indicate that public-private partnering among governmental, nongovernmental and commercial organizations is a matter of perseverance and vigor.

8.5   DEEPENING THE THEORETICAL BASIS

The review of the literature supports the prominent position of public-private partnerships in the creation of next sustainable practice for industry.

Von Malmborg (2003) substantiates that organizations that engage in a public-private partnership for sustainable development and thus take the lead in developing the nation's next sustainable practice can have a range of qualities. They must be willing and knowledgably competent partners with patience and a feeling for the pitfalls, hidden agendas, interests and specific organizational cultures of the organizations they engage with as partners. They also must be able to translate a rather broad vision of sustainable development into workable programs and action plans. The objectives of the public-private partnership must be realistic to the partnering organizations. Partners have to be competent in the organizational aspect as well as the substance of the sustainable public-private partnership. If they do not have these competences, either managerial competence or sustainable knowledge should be hired from outside to neutralize this deficiency. With respect to the concept of the public-private partnership, Von Malmborg (2003) demonstrates that the social aspect is important. People who represent a governmental, nongovernmental or commercial organization need to be able to build trust and cooperate on the basis of that trust. They must have sufficient managerial and interpersonal skills, be able to identify their knowledge deficiencies and act on this, for example by hiring experts from the outside.

Krozer, Mass and Kothuis (2003), Harborne and Hendry (2009) and Hendry, Harborne and Brown (2010) contend that there are serious impediments to the diffusion of innovative practices from public-private partnerships to other firms in industry. They argue that this failure is caused by a lack of incentives. Most firms in industry do not participate in a public-private partnership. Most of them may not even look at the next practices that are developed by public-private partnerships and instead go on with their traditional practice. It is their comfort zone. In addition, for next practices, especially sustainable practices, the financial parameters are precarious. That is not a comfort zone but a danger zone. Firms, for example, want to know whether savings and earnings during the lifetime of a production plant or production process will compensate for the investments required. Most firms, small and medium-size firms in particular, are preoccupied with short-term actions that are related to low-cost strategies and price competition in today's markets, not so much with next sustainable practices for the longer term. The sustainable market of the future can, for many firms, be too far away to invest in. Keoleian and Kar (2003) and Krozer, Mass and Kothuis (2003) argue that diffusion of next practices from public-private partnerships to industry can be supported by educating and training industry and by informing them about the possibilities and opportunities of next sustainable practices. People can, for instance, be taught how to apply environmental and safety management systems that are based on norms of the International Standardization Organization (ISO), such as the ISO 14000 norm series (see Appendices 2, 3, 4, 5 and 6) and the ISO 26000 norm (see Appendix 7). Firms can be informed of how much customers, in both business-to-business and business-to-consumer markets, start to ask for these systems. Although direct diffusion from public-private partnerships to the majority of firms is not always taking place, indirect changes in industry can be induced by public-private partnerships that promote next practices. Tomorrow's regulation, for example, can change in favor of next practice. Or, tomorrow's subsidy programs can be oriented toward firms, nongovernmental organizations, research centers and knowledge workers who act in the spirit of the next practice. Next practice thus has the potential to change the playing field on which organizations have to compete. This implies that the firm is not an entity that is isolated from its business environment. It is part of it and has to put efforts in serving stakeholders. It therefore has to choose when and how to adopt aspects of demonstrated next practice. Krozer, Mass and Kothuis (2003), Harborne and Hendry (2009) and Hendry, Harborne and Brown (2010) maintain that public-private demonstrations have a considerable effect on industry, not so much in terms of direct diffusion as in terms of changing regulation, market demand and national policy.

Ählström and Sjöström (2005) argue that nongovernmental organizations can be valuable partners in a public-private partnership but that not all nongovernmental organizations are helpful and cooperative by nature. They underpin their argument by distinguishing so-called preserving, protesting, modifying and scrutinizing nongovernmental organizations. According to Ählström and Sjöström (2005), preservers have a partnership strategy and try to do cooperative projects, education and joint marketing with governments and the private sector. But protesters hang on to an independency strategy and focus on acting against the existing world by means of protest campaigns and protest actions. Modifiers also hang on to their independency and choose not to cooperate with government and business. Modifying nongovernmental organizations want to realize a paradigm shift in corporate practice. They refuse to cooperate because they do not want to give in on their paradigm and act by means of demonstrations and publications to disseminate their new scenarios. Finally, scrutinizers also refuse to cooperate and want to stay independent. They plan to influence corporate behavior by highlighting what they believe firms are doing wrong. They influence public opinion about this by media attention. Ählström and

Table 8.1   Frame of Reference for Eco-innovative and Sustainable Public-Private Partnerships

Public-private partnerships	Characteristics
Governmental push	Public-private partnerships are guided by governmental sustainable policy plans, are dependent on the political climate and stability of the country's government, are guided by (inter)national rules, laws and codes of conduct, have difficulties with norms that are complex and that differ from country to country, are guided by financial incentives and obstacles, are sensitive to customer demand that is changing in favor of sustainability, know that sustainability can become an element that provides future competitive advantage.
Agreements	Public-private partnerships are guided by oral and written agreements between partners, are guided by codes of conduct, are managed, coordinated and staffed by people with excellent managerial, social and negotiation skills.
Next-practice creation	Public-private partnerships develop next practices for industry, have the form of an R&D consortium that develops new standards or have the form of a demonstration project that shows to industry what the next practice can be.

Sjöström's (2005) classification sheds an interesting light on nongovernmental organizations' intentions and ambitions. Most of these nongovernmental organizations probably do not intend to change the world by means of joining a public-private partnership. It seems that the only willing nongovernmental organizations that join public-private partnerships to develop next sustainable practice are the preservers. The others apply different strategies to change the world.

The research in this chapter indicates that the public-private partnership is a powerful organizational form for the development of an industry's next sustainable practice. The frame of reference in Table 8.1 shows the characteristics of eco-innovative and sustainable public-private partnerships. The government can use policy plans, financial incentives and regulation to support the public-private initiatives. The partnering commercial, governmental and nongovernmental organizations can use a broad spectrum of management methods, social skills and negotiation skills to manage a public-private partnership and create industry's next eco- and sustainably innovative practice.

The research in this chapter indicates that the characteristics of sustainable public-private partnerships can contribute to the transformation of sustainably innovative ideas, concepts, visions and initiatives into innovative next sustainable practice in industry.

8.6 SUMMARY

The public-private partnership is the fourth element at the co-innovation level of the model of eco-innovation and sustainability management. The research shows that the sustainably innovative public-private partnership creates and demonstrates industry's next practice. A cadre of governmental policy plans, regulations and financial incentives enables governmental, non-governmental and commercial organizations to team up in R&D consortia and demonstration projects. In these experimental organizational settings, the organizations join forces to create the next practice for the nation's industry. The eco- and sustainably innovative public-private partnership is an important organizational form that structures co-innovative activity.

This co-innovation process is located in the sphere of the co-institutionalization process, which provides the infrastructural arrangements for innovative businesses and practices to grow large. The co-institutionalization level of the model of eco- and sustainable innovation is the subject of the next three chapters. The next chapter starts with the first element at this level, which is market and society.

9 Co-institutionalization by Market and Society

The first category of factors at the co-institutionalization level is the category of market and society. Market demand is a crucial factor in the process of industrial change. When market demands change, this can cause complete new businesses to develop and new industries to arise. When public opinion changes and new issues are put on the societal agenda, this can be the start of fundamental industrial change. Industry has to react and adapt to what happens in its business environment, and since most businesses exist and survive because of sufficient market demand and societal support, they need to keep up with changes in markets and societies. A key characteristic of market and societal change with respect to eco-innovation and sustainability is that these aspects are increasingly becoming business-qualifying and business-winning factors. Sustainability is becoming a driver behind new business and behind the rejuvenation of traditional industry. Market and societal influence on business performance thus can be significant. Business's classic economic approach is to meet the explicit or latent needs of customers, from the need for food, water, clothes, shelter and transport to that for entertainment and personal development. In the past, this approach has resulted in mass industrialization and in the mass production and consumption of food, drinks, clothing, dwellings, cars, aircrafts, buses, bikes and trains, jewelry, fashion, art, motion pictures and media. A recent trend is that market and societal awareness of sustainability has become integrated into this classical approach. It adds a fundamental aspect to traditional business and forces business to start thinking about how to serve all the existing needs of consumers and make a profit, while simultaneously addressing sustainability issues. Suddenly firms have to ask themselves questions about the eco-effectiveness and -efficiency of their production processes, products and supply chains. Nevertheless, just asking these questions will not be sufficient. Firms are also required to come up with answers and solutions. Changing forces and demands in market and society stimulate organizations at the co-innovation level to move their perhaps rather tiny eco- and sustainably innovative businesses toward mass

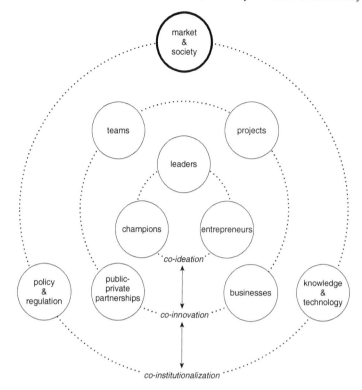

Figure 9.1 Co-institutionalization by market and society.

production and consumption. Market and society are the first element at the co-institutionalization level of the model of eco-innovation and sustainability management (see Figure 9.1).

This chapter first presents theory that forms the basis of the market and society element of the model (Section 9.2). It then describes the methods that are used to explore the analytical validity of this element for industry (Section 9.3). It continues with an exploration of the analytical value of the market and society element in practice (Section 9.4) and in theory (Section 9.5). It concludes with a summary (Section 9.6).

9.2 THEORETICAL BASIS

In the past industrial decades, markets and society were, as they still are, organized in accordance with the virtual concept of abundance. Production systems function as if finite natural resources are infinite. Markets and societies are organized around the mass production of goods and services. The creed is "as much as possible, as efficiently as possible and as effectively as possible," with turnover and profit maximization as the main goals. Most natural resources, such as fossil energy resources and natural materials, are finite, but the industrial production and consumption systems and patterns do not integrate this into their accounting and mental procedures. In recent years, it seems that markets and society are becoming aware that this approach is unsustainable and will not be tenable for the industrial decades to come. In a new, sustainable industrial era, the societal costs of the use of finite resources may need to be integrated into the economic system, while the benefits of the use and reuse of infinite resources can be integrated, too. How this all is changing for the better is not sure, but it seems that markets and society are increasingly asking for changes that will move industry toward new sustainable accounting and mental systems.

Market Change

In the literature, the concept of changing markets and markets that induce industrial innovation is commonly accepted. Market change can be the driver of innovation, but when market demand is stable and asks for the same products, markets are also drivers of repetition and invariability. Sustainability, green thinking and eco-awareness are often not in the DNA of the average customer, and it seems that most people still do not know what these concepts are or can be. Sheth, Sethia and Srinivas (2011) address the influence of customer demand in their work, which takes a customer-centered approach to sustainability. They document that the effectiveness of industry in dealing with sustainability will define its success in the near future. Their argument is based on the concept that sustainability is multi-dimensional and integrates environmental, social and economic elements. They concentrate on the relation between the consumer and sustainability and introduce the concept of customer-centric sustainability, which they define as "the consumption-mediated impact of marketing actions on environmental, personal and economic well-being of the consumer" (p. 24). In this definition, the economic well-being of the consumer is defined as the "health and human well-being consequences of environmental change ensuing from consumption" (p. 24); the personal well-being of the consumer is "individual well-being or quality of life, and associated welfare of the community" (p. 24); and the economic well-being of the consumer is defined as the "financial aspects such as debt-burden, earning pressures, and work-life balance" (p. 24). According to Sheth, Sethia and Srinivas (2011), a key challenge for business is to serve all these types of explicit and latent aspects of customers' demand for well-being. The goal of green production and consumption should be to sell and buy products and services with an environmental footprint over their total life cycle that can be carried by the earth. Sheth, Sethia and Srinivas (2011) continue that although consumers increasingly say that they want to buy and consume sustainable products and services, the market shares of sustainably produced products and services remain relatively low. With growing populations and growing numbers of people who want their share of consumption, the environmental burden on a global scale will keep on growing. Even relatively popular eco-innovative and sustainable products, such as hybrid cars, organic food and green detergents, have modest market shares, below 10 percent worldwide. The authors conclude that sustainable consumption may be necessary but has not yet been realized. A robust change in market demand and consumption patterns toward sustainability can be accelerated by the adoption of what Sheth, Sethia and Srinivas (2011) call "mindful consumption." Mindfully consuming people take account, in thought and behavior, of the consequences of their consumption habits and patterns. Mindful consumption can change customers' perception of products and services in favor of sustainable, tempered and high-quality consumption. Sheth, Sethia and Srinivas (2011) contend that the well-known four Ps of marketing—product, price, promotion and place—can be useful concepts to make buying behavior and people's consumption patterns more sustainable. Products, for example, can be designed to make them more durable. Price can be used to regulate use, for example, if the price of unsustainable products and services is increased. Promotion can be used to inform the consumer about the superior quality of sustainable products and services through advertising and communication strategies. Finally, the place element of marketing can be used by creating service centers that provide easy access to the repair and reuse of products.

Societal Change

Society seems to be increasingly aware that it has to solve environmental, social and societal problems in the coming decades. This awareness is influenced by studies and publications of prominent international taskforces and prominent officials. The Club of Rome (Meadows, 1972), the World Commission on Environment and Development (Brundtland and Khalid, 1987), the United Nations Conference on Environment and Development (UNCED, 1992) and, recently, Al Gore (Gore, 2006) have proclaimed that natural resources are exhaustible, that the earth's capacity to renew itself is finite and that natural balance can and will be disturbed and maybe even irreversibly and dangerously changed (see also Carson, 1962; Hawken, 1993; Lovelock, 1980). In recent decades, people's awareness of possible environmental dilemmas has seemed to be growing. Environmental problems, such as climate change, loss of biodiversity and the depletion of natural resources, are becoming issues on the agendas of many countries' governments, industrial consortia and societal interest groups (Paramanathan, Farrukh, Phaal and Probert, 2004).

Dominant international issues of environmental sustainability are the change of substance cycles, the depletion of raw material sources, the depletion of finite energy resources, climate change, acidification of the atmosphere, the drying of surface and soil and the degradation of biodiversity (Blackburn, 2007; Esty, Levy, Srebotnjak and Sherbinin, 2005). First, the problem of changing substance cycles is caused by human activity. Human activity accelerates natural substance flows and puts new flows of substances in motion. Because there is insufficient control of the cycling of materials from extraction to use to possible reuse to final disposal, substances are emitted into the environment at the wrong time, in the wrong place and in the wrong form. Concomitantly, the pollution problem arises, and waste builds up. Second, the depletion of raw material sources can be a problem because of the finiteness of the commodity stocks of the earth. Single use of raw materials and then their designation as waste can lead to a rapid depletion of the earth's inventory of raw materials. Third, the possible problem of the depletion of energy resources is a consequence of the finiteness of fossil fuel stocks. Most current energy consumption is still based on the use of fossil fuels. If no solutions are devised, energy shortage may be a consequence. Solutions can be sought by using infinite energy sources such as wind and solar energy. Fourth, the possible problems that are related to global warming can be major. The prevailing view is that emissions of carbon dioxide (CO_2) contribute to the emergence and further increase of global warming, the so-called greenhouse hazard. Industry is also causing this problem. For example during production and transportation of materials, CO_2 is emitted into the environment. Fifth, acidification of the atmosphere can lead to damage to forests, natural areas, cultural areas and drinking water because of the emission of chemicals such as sulfur dioxide (SO_2), nitrogen oxide (NO_x) and ammonia (NH_3). These substances are released during the production and application of various materials used in production processes. Sixth, the drying of surface and soil represents the possible problems associated with maintaining surface water and groundwater. The consumption of water in various areas is not always adapted to the abilities of surface water sources and groundwater sources in the immediate vicinity. Seventh, the degradation of biodiversity includes possible problems related to the extinction of species and other organisms. Organisms release oxygen and nutrients, contribute to degradation of waste and provide for regeneration of soil. They also facilitate material cycles in which pollutants are converted into harmless substances or substances that are of service for the further development of the environment. The extinction of organisms or a disturbance of the relationships between types of organisms can have a debilitating influence on the ecological basis for the well-being of humans.

9.3   RESEARCH METHOD

Additional empirical and theoretical studies are performed to further increase the analytical value of the market and society element of the model of eco-innovation and sustainability management for industry.

Step 1. Shaping the Research Model

This chapter builds on the results from the initial study of Bossink (2011a) (see Appendix 1). It focuses on the market and society element of the model (Section 9.2) and conducts empirical research in various Dutch industries to study how the market and society element of the model holds for other empirical contexts (Section 9.4). It carries out a literature review of the influence of market and society on sustainable industry in order to explore how this element of the model can be shaped toward a broader analytical value for industry (Section 9.5).

Step 2. Conducting Theoretical and Empirical Studies

Literature databases are consulted for research papers on the influence of market and society on environmental, ecological, green, social, societal, biological and sustainably innovative initiatives in industry. In addition to this, thirty managers and experts in various Dutch industries are interviewed and asked to reflect on the influence of market and society on sustainability issues (Indriani, 2009).

Step 3. Analyzing and Synthesizing the Studies' Outcomes

The market and society element in the initial model (Bossink, 2011a) is confronted with the additional empirical and theoretical studies. On the basis of the outcomes of this analysis, the characteristics of the market and society element at the co-institutionalization level are articulated for industry (Section 9.5).

9.4 EXPLORING THE EMPIRICAL FIELD

The exploratory interviews indicate that market and societal demand is changing in favor of eco-innovation and sustainability but that this change is taking place relatively slowly. Respondents confirm that once consumers and society perceive sustainability as a quality aspect that increases the value of products and services, markets for sustainably produced goods can grow steadily. This section is the author's interpretation of Indriani (2009), and quotations are taken from that source.

Market Change

A challenge for business is to provide superior product and service performance to customers on the basis of ecological, social and societal features. Various respondents think that this is not easy. From the perspective of a consumer, the first question is what a product or service can do for him or her. The question what it does to others is maybe important but is not the primary question of many consumers. One of the respondents articulates this as follows: "I do believe—and that applies to all products—that consumers decide on quality and price, and very little on environmental and social aspects" (p. 38). The challenge for business therefore is to articulate the sustainable aspects of their production processes and products and services in terms of the primary quality perception of the consumer. This, for example, means that a cleaner car can be sold to the customer as a cheaper car. If a cleaner car is not cheaper but instead is more expensive, it can be upgraded by extraordinary design and image that appeals to the primary buying behavior of the customer. On the other hand, some of the respondents are convinced that the customer is increasingly aware of sustainability; they think that when two products are identical, many customers will choose the more sustainable product. The problem is that the sustainability scores of most products are not transparent, and when they are transparent, it is not clear how these scores compare to the scores of competing products. This is clearly explained by a respondent who thinks that "sustainability is important for most consumers, but I also think that a lot of consumers do not know what sustainability is. The role of the government and companies here is to inform consumers; to inform them about the advantages of environmentally friendly products or services" (p. 40). This implies that latent customer awareness can be triggered and served by business. Despite this, the respondents' answers indicate that they are not sure whether large consumer market segments will buy and use sustainably produced products and services. It may be that just a relatively small market segment is willing to pay a higher price for a product of premium (sustainable) quality. An interviewee, for example, says that "perhaps 5 to 10 percent of all consumers are very interested [in sustainable products] and willing to pay more, another 15 to 20 percent are interested but not willing to pay more . . . most consumers do not want to pay more" (p. 44). This suggests that marketing strategies of firms may need to target each segment differently and with different mixes of pricing, product features and promotion activities. In addition, respondents state that business not only should improve communication about sustainably improved products but also has to develop and design radically new sustainable products that outperform the old products. One of the interviewees in this respect, for example, states that "it is difficult to compete with existing products. . . . You should really have something new" (p. 46). Consumers tend to use and stick to traditional products they are used to, but at the same time they adopt new products and services because this can be psychologically exciting and rewarding.

Societal Change

Firms are increasingly aware of the opportunities of changing societal demands and of changes in public opinions. Most multinational firms dedicate a chapter in their annual reports to sustainability and corporate social responsibility. Moreover, they appoint corporate sustainability directors who have to develop the corporate sustainability policy of the firm. Firms know that society expects them to transform into sustainable firms. They thus change operations, analyze their value chains and supply chains to look what can be improved and communicate to stakeholders what exactly has been changed and what that means to society in terms of the firm's ecological footprint. Firms can invest in societal development, for example, by donating to a nongovernmental organization like the World Wild Fund for Nature (WWF) or by introducing eco-certificates and eco-labels for their products (for more about eco-labeling, see Appendix 4). With respect to these eco-certificates and eco-labels, an interviewee says that his firm, a Dutch multinational in the food industry, has "several initiatives. We certify sustainable agriculture [and in cooperation with several other multinationals] cooperate directly with suppliers" (p. 46) to improve sustainability throughout the production chain. Respondents perceive an eco-label as a means to appeal to the latent needs of customers for sustainable quality. One of the respondents states that eco-labels provide "information on the packaging about the environmental issues concerned. The CO_2 label is an extensive label. It qualifies the amount of CO_2 emissions per unit of production. Another label is a so-called 'airplane logo' on products. This label comes from the debate on food miles; there should be as little as possible" (p. 47). Interviewees agree on the influence of popular media on societal awareness with regard to sustainability and eco-innovation. Media attention to social phenomena such as obesity, food quality and toxicity of packaging informs society and triggers industry to protect their business. While this can be taken care of with lawsuits and other defensive reactions, respondents comment that their firms want to take the route of business improvement. They, for example, reduce the number of calories in their food products to fight obesity. An interviewee from a nongovernmental organization observed that "we published an article, which proclaimed that [obesity] also is a responsibility of industry. . . . The next day we got a phone-call from [a multinational food company]" (p. 58) that wanted to cooperate and work with us on solutions. This is an example of societal change and its influence on business. This process of give and take, action and reaction and question and answer between society and business can be a driver of increasing sustainable business. The interviews indicate that firms interact with society and that this interaction results in ongoing business and societal change.

9.5 DEEPENING THE THEORETICAL BASIS

The review of the literature further uncovers the prominent position of changing customer behavior and societal awareness as factors that contribute to the institutionalization of eco-innovative and sustainable practice.

Prothero, McDonagh and Dobscha (2010) argue that consumers' motives for buying sustainable, green or eco-innovative products and services have certain constant characteristics and that green consumers can be categorized. Prothero, McDonagh and Dobscha (2010) introduce a typology of four consumer types. Their first category is the so-called blind green consumer. The blind green consumer buys green products because they provide certain benefits, which do not have to be related to the sustainability aspect. Self-interest is the main motivation to buy. To this type of consumers, sustainability is not a priority. Other issues are more important, such as cost savings. The blind green consumer, for example, reuses goods because this saves money. The next type of consumer is the individual green citizen. The individual green citizen is environmentally aware and buys products and services for reasons of self-interest that directly relate to the sustainability aspect. The sustainability aspect of the product or service provides the buyer a desired experience and feeling. Such a consumer type buys organic food, for example meat from chickens that had plenty of space in a natural environment and were not imprisoned in a breeding plant. They buy this because they believe it is healthful. The third consumer type is the collective green consumer. The collective green consumer is driven by the awareness that buying behavior can have a large impact on society. The collective green consumer is motivated by concern for the common interest. This consumer type knows that buying behavior can have an influence on environmental issues. It can change industry and change environmental footprints. For example, this consumer may buy an electric car and, by doing so, try to contribute to a change in the automobile industry. The fourth type of customers is the collective green citizen. The collective green citizen is, like the collective green consumer, interested in contributing to industrial change toward sustainability, but in this case not by means of buying. The collective green citizen focuses on *not* buying, on reuse and redistribution and on alternative types of consumption. Collective green citizens want to reduce their dependence on buying patterns and the associated production systems and act to develop new alternative systems that are less unsustainable. An example is a person who buys clothes from a secondhand store. Prothero, McDonagh and Dobscha's (2010) typology provides insights into how to appeal to consumers' needs and mental patterns that direct buying behavior. Governmental, nongovernmental and commercial organizations can, for example, orient their communication and promotion campaigns to these different types of consumers. Product development and design in firms can integrate aspects that fit with one or more of these consumer types. They do not require that consumers change. They suggest that business activity can change by appealing to consumers' needs and, by doing so, change industry.

Steurer and Konrad (2009) present several guidelines for firms' corporate social responsibility policy. According to Steurer and Konrad (2009), corporate responsibility means that firms have economic, social and environmental responsibilities. They state that economic responsibility drives a firm

Table 9.1 Frame of Reference for Market and Society's Influence on Eco- and Sustainable Innovation in Industry

Market and society	Characteristics
Market change	Market changes can stimulate firms to produce products and services that contribute to consumers' well-being, can stimulate firms to reduce their environmental footprints, may ask firms to come with sustainable products that appeal to consumers' primary as well as latent needs.
Societal change	Societal changes can stimulate firms to contribute to international sustainability issues (e.g., change of substance cycles, depletion of raw material sources, depletion of finite energy resources, climate change, acidification of the atmosphere, drying of surface and soil and degradation of biodiversity), can stimulate firms to care for society, can stimulate firms to take responsibility for sustainability.

"to perform in a way that enables the company to continue for an indefinite time" (p. 27). The firm thus must secure its financial performance, long-term perspectives and economic impacts. This can be taken care of by generating sufficient cash flow, turnover and profits. This economic aspect has a sustainable side. It implies that the firm must be competitive in the sense that it is durable. It must have an economic impact on various stakeholders if it is to survive in the long term. Steurer and Konrad (2009) contend that a firm's social responsibility is "to contribute to the social well-being of the society and individuals" (p. 27). With respect to this, they elaborate on the concept and meaning of "equity" and distinguish among several types of equity. Firms, for example, can target an equal distribution of income within the firm. Moreover, the firm can contribute to good and improved social conditions inside and outside the firm. In addition to this, Steurer and Konrad (2009) define a firm's environmental responsibility as its obligation "to maintain natural capital to a certain (paradigm specific) degree" (p. 27). This definition implies that the sustainable paradigm or basic principle a firm chooses determines how and why natural capital is maintained. Steurer and Konrad (2009) write that firms must be transparent and report and communicate their sustainable performance. They have to be reflexive and open to suggestions from the outside world to repair environmental damage they have caused. Progress on this must be reported, evaluated and monitored.

The research in this chapter indicates that market and society are powerful dynamic forces and drivers behind institutionalization of sustainable innovation in industry. Market and societal changes put pressure on and provide incentives for firms to generate substantive sustainable business.

The frame of reference in Table 9.1 shows the characteristics of market and societal forces that drive eco- and sustainable innovation.

The research in this chapter indicates that market and society can stimulate organizations to grow their eco- and sustainably innovative business toward mass production and consumption.

9.6 SUMMARY

Market and society are the first element at the co-institutionalization level of the model of eco-innovation and sustainability. The research shows that market and societal change can induce firms to adapt and become eco-innovative and sustainable. When market change and societal change are in favor of eco-innovation and sustainability, they can stimulate firms to strengthen their sustainable initiatives. They can inspire niche players that focus on specialized markets to transform into mass producers of sustainable products and services. Market and society are an important institutional factor that can enable sustainably innovating firms to grow large, conquer the market and change industry. The second important factor at the co-institutionalization level is knowledge and technology. This is the subject of the next chapter.

10 Co-institutionalization by Knowledge and Technology

10.1 INTRODUCTION

The second category of factors at the co-institutionalization level is the category of knowledge and technology. Knowledge and technology are often perceived as a main source of innovation. Knowledge and technology can enable inventions, new designs, production processes and marketing activities. Technological development can push customers into new directions. Today's industry seems to be on the threshold of being part of a sustainable society, a society that is based on recycling of materials, sustainable aesthetics and environmental philosophies of product usage, use of infinite energy sources and clean production processes. Technological development is an ongoing process in modern society, and firms are part of this process. Large multinational firms are continuously seeking new products and services that will provide turnover for the next couple of years. In addition to having their own research laboratories, they can also invest in relationships with universities and gain access to professors and academic research staff. They can form R&D consortia in which firms, authorities and universities bundle resources to develop knowledge and technology in fundamental and applied areas. In modern Western industry, knowledge flows from firm to government to university and vice versa. These knowledge-transfer processes provide university researchers with the latest insights into societal needs and demands. It enables the government to fund research that has societal urgency. These knowledge-transfer processes give firms the opportunity to develop future markets and to contribute to large-scale delivery of new sustainable technologies. With respect to sustainability, there can be a growing need for an integration of eco-innovative and sustainable thinking in existing and new product- and service-production processes. Ongoing knowledge production and technological development stimulate organizations at the co-innovation level to grow their eco- and sustainably innovative businesses toward mass production and consumption. Knowledge and technology are the second element at the co-institutionalization level of the model of eco-innovation and sustainability management (see Figure 10.1)

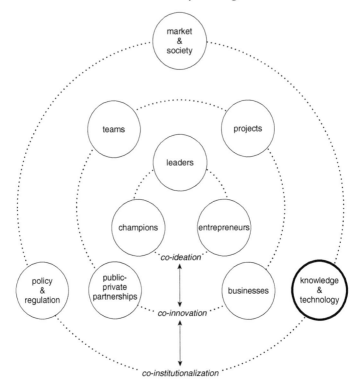

Figure 10.1   Co-institutionalization by knowledge and technology.

This chapter organizes the theory that forms the basis of the knowledge and technology element of the model (Section 10.2). It describes the methods that are used to explore the analytical validity of this element for industry (Section 10.3). Then it explores the analytical value of this element in practice (Section 10.4) and in theory (Section 10.5). It concludes with a summary (Section 10.6).

10.2   THEORETICAL BASIS

Nations and firms invest substantial amounts of money in R&D and in the development of new products, processes and services that provide welfare and well-being to society and financial profits to shareholders. A classical organizational form of national R&D is that fundamental research into natural and social sciences is located in universities and that research groups and laboratories that seek opportunities to apply knowledge and develop new applications and products are located in public-private partnerships and in commercial firms. Today's national organization of R&D is less strict and more diffuse in the sense that firms also conduct fundamental research and universities also concentrate on the applied and product developmental side of science. In addition to this, universities and firms tend to develop more intense and close cooperation in R&D consortia in which fundamental and commercial research are mixed to directly serve market and society.

Knowledge Flow

A nation needs multiple knowledge bases to structure and nurture innovation processes. Governments and companies can get access to the necessary knowledge bases through networking attempts and information-exchange activities of their people (Blindenbach-Driessen and Van den Ende, 2006; Brennan and Dooley, 2005; Chesbrough, 2010; Von Zedtwitz and Gassmann, 2002). Innovative companies are often part of knowledge networks that transcend the boundaries of their departments, organizations and industrial sector. Regular contacts with specialists in their networks keep the firms' people informed of the latest developments in technology, markets and society. In this context, Goverse, Hekkert, Groenewegen, Worrell and Smits (2001) underpin the immense innovative potential of knowledge networks that consist of universities, research institutes and knowledge-intensive firms. They demonstrate that the flow of knowledge among these actors facilitates the development of new knowledge and contend that this continuous process of knowledge generation has a positive influence on innovative activity. Furthermore, Seaden and Manseau (2001) stress the positive effect of programs that promote loose, informal collaborative arrangements and information exchange between organizations. R&D can be a part of the daily job of all employees. People can be triggered to frequently contact each other and talk about "the story of the day," hear about the latest trends, share insights about changes in market demand and customer preferences and maintain an innovative mindset. In the literature, information exchange is frequently mentioned as one of the important stimuli of innovation (Dammann and Elle, 2006; Gluch and Stenberg, 2006). An innovative organization shares and exchanges information with the outside world. It gathers information about what is happening and, equally important, lets the world know what is happening with and within the firm. It enables other companies to decide whether the firm is an interesting partner to work with, to have ties with or to buy from. Toole (1998), for example, argues that manufacturers and retailers that provide information to their business clients about the new products in their portfolios increase the likelihood that these will be sold. In line with this, Veshosky (1998) explores the information-seeking behavior of managers and finds that innovative firms facilitate their managers to obtain information and to communicate with members of their outside networks. For these contacts and exchange of knowledge, it can be necessary that a substantial group of people speak a common language. Dammann and Elle (2006) contend that when firms in an industry have the same understanding of the area in which they innovate, this has a positive influence on their innovative performance. In most industries, the loose and lateral communication structures of projects and organizations can facilitate the exchange of information and the development of knowledge that is needed to innovate (Barlow, 2000).

Technological Drive

Technological progress can be a source for firms' innovative activity and can push customers to buy new products and services that result from this innovation activity. Innovative firms that have the capability to absorb new technological knowledge from their environment and apply this knowledge to improve and renew their products and services can offer new alternatives to the outside world (Cohen and Levinthal, 1990). One concept that enables companies to innovate is the concept of combination and recombination (Orihata and Watanabe, 2000). This concept means that companies connect and assemble existing and new knowledge and technology and, by doing so, realize a continuous stream of innovative products and services. A company's capability to combine and recombine knowledge and technology can contribute to the company's innovative strength. Kangari and Miyatake (1997), for instance, investigate the factors that contribute to the development of innovative technology by firms. They find that many technology-oriented firms focus mainly on the integration of diverse technologies from various disciplines. In other words, they combine and recombine, and that is their primary way to develop new business. Firms that operate a (re) combination technology strategy need a sound technological basis to be capable of absorbing new technological knowledge (Cohen and Levinthal, 1990). Many lower-tech or no-tech firms do not own such a technology and knowledge base and may need a broker or a meeting platform to gain access to technological firms with which to cooperate. In this context, Goverse, Hekkert, Groenewegen, Worrell and Smits (2001) and Seaden and Manseau (2001) stress the importance of national or regional stimulation programs and of bridging institutions that enable organizations to get access to the technology they need to innovate. In addition to this, Miozzo and Dewick (2002) argue that long-term relations between firms and external knowledge centers can be a necessary coordination mechanism to, for example, facilitate access to appropriate technologies. Kangari and Miyatake (1997) argue that a firm can achieve prominence through strategies that are based on technological competence. The combination of a firm's technological competences and its ability to (re)combine can be a powerful foundation for a technology strategy. New market demands are often triggered by new technology-based offerings. Mitropoulos and Tatum (2000) argue in this context that technological solutions developed by innovators often precede the problems they are going to solve. Advanced technology can shape the demands of the client, and the technological capabilities of leading organizations can be a source of innovative activity.

Design for Sustainability

New sustainable knowledge and technology can be integrated into the design of new products (see also Appendix 6). Donnelly, Olds, Blechinger, Reynolds and Beckett-Furnell (2004) introduce a method to integrate sustainability into the design processes of firms. They argue that new sustainable products have to be developed because of market needs or ideas that are powerful enough to create new markets. In the stage of developing, the environmental requirements and specifications of the new product concept have to be taken into account. The product ideas and blueprints are, for example, subject to environmental laws, regulation and standards, customer demands and the firm's own sustainability policy, goals and standards. In addition to this, a firm has to develop a so-called eco-roadmap. In an eco-roadmap, the company assesses what sustainability features the product must have and how these can be realized by changing the composition of the product. In the next stage, the firm translates design specifications into prototypes and design reviews and develops designs that can be manufactured. In this stage, the company has to apply "design-for-environment" procedures in which the designers evaluate the environmental concerns of parts and elements of the product design, including energy efficiency, environmental hazardous substances and recyclability. The designers, for example, use standardized forms, guidelines and checklists to methodologically conduct an environmental assessment (see also Appendix 5). Donnelly, Olds, Blechinger, Reynolds and Beckett-Furnell's (2004) method enables the integration of environmental knowledge and technology in the product design processes of the firm.

10.3   RESEARCH METHOD

Additional empirical and theoretical studies are performed to further increase the analytical value of the knowledge and technology element of the model of eco-innovation and sustainability management for industry.

Step 1.   Shaping the Research Model

This chapter builds on the results from the initial study of Bossink (2011a) (see Appendix 1). It focuses on the knowledge and technology element of the model (Section 10.2) and conducts empirical research in the Dutch food industry to study how the knowledge and technology element of the model holds for another empirical setting (Section 10.4). It carries out a literature review of the influence of knowledge and technology on the sustainable innovativeness of industry to explore how this element of the model can be shaped toward a broader analytical value for industry (Section 10.5).

Step 2.   Conducting Theoretical and Empirical Studies

Literature databases are consulted for research papers on the influence of knowledge and technology on environmental, ecological, green, social, societal, biological and sustainably innovative initiatives in industry. In addition to this, ten managers and experts in the Dutch food industry are interviewed and asked to elaborate on the influence of knowledge and technology on sustainable innovation in their industry (De Swaaf, 2008).

Step 3.   Analyzing and Synthesizing the Studies' Outcomes

The knowledge and technology element in the initial model (Bossink, 2011a) is confronted with the additional empirical and theoretical studies. On the basis of the outcomes of this analysis, the characteristics of the knowledge and technology element at the co-institutionalization level are articulated for industry (Section 10.5).

10.4   EXPLORING THE EMPIRICAL FIELD

The exploratory interviews indicate that today's knowledge and technological development is increasingly directed toward eco-innovation and sustainability. Respondents confirm that the flow of knowledge and technology among universities and other research centers, governments, nongovernmental organizations and commercial firms contributes to a context in which sustainable innovation can flourish. This section is the author's interpretation by De Swaaf (2008), and quotations are taken from that source.

Knowledge Flow

Respondents agree that open innovation routines are important. An open structure in which high-tech firms, suppliers, startup companies and academic research groups cooperate can be a source of innovation and renewal. This can be organized in so-called science cities, incubator areas, innovation clusters, networks or high-tech valleys. In a geographic area, firms, knowledge workers, investors and governmental officials can come together to work on promising new business proposals and to develop new innovations. Such a structure can be established and be used to enforce the innovativeness of a region or, on a larger scale, a country's innovativeness. One of the respondents, for example, draws the following picture: "The big firms are in the center of the action and around them all kinds of small, perky satellite start-ups circulate. The moment these satellites discover something new and valuable they sell themselves to the big firms, and these are going to put it on the market. Last week I visited a [Dutch science park]. On the site, where a few years ago a major research facility was located that operated under secrecy and was closed for visitors, today forty to fifty high-tech firms operate and these firms are constantly exchanging knowledge" (p. 166). The dynamics of knowledge exchange between firms and their agents can be seen as an innovation-driving factor in an industry on both a regional and a national level. In the Dutch food industry, it is important to continuously develop new product versions, and therefore cooperation with different organizations can be important. One of the representatives of a firm in the food industry remarks: "We need more than ties with universities. Nowadays many domains are important. It is difficult to form R&D consortia with several firms and knowledge centers, but it is necessary. We do it all the time" (p. 166). To commercialize a new product idea on a national scale, cooperation with many firms such as market research bureaus and consultancy firms is important.

Technological Drive

Although in past years secret innovation laboratories developed into open innovation networks, firms and other participants in the innovation networks think it is difficult to open up to others completely. There always is a competitive drive between companies and their employees and between universities and academic researchers. An interviewee puts it this way: "For scientists it is difficult to work outside their domains. Scientists have to write proposals to obtain funding for their own research projects. That is how our system works. How often do you as a researcher involve people from other organizations once you obtained funding? It is not common practice to do that. We should let specialists from other organizations in more often. To develop the best technology you need the best combinations of specialists and thus specialists from different organizations" (pp. 166–167). The source for technological development can be found in various organizations and in combining knowledge and expertise from these organizations. An interviewee, for example, states that specialists working on new products have complementary competences that should be combined: "Not all R&D specialists have a drive to design for energy-efficiency" (p. 187). In that case, it is important to team up with one or more specialists who know how to do that. The interviews indicate that technological development can be stimulated by crossing organizational and industrial boundaries.

Design for Sustainability

In the design stage of new-product-development processes in firms, designers decide which types of materials to use and what energy conversion techniques to apply. In the design stage, sustainable solutions can be integrated with far-reaching consequences that transcend the boundaries of organizations. R&D, production processes and mass distribution channels of various firms are often linked and are all part of the same chain of production and consumption. A respondent, for example, plainly says: "Yes, a solution for an environmental problem can be found in another industrial sector. One must not separate industrial sectors" (p. 176). This interviewee has clear ideas about the importance of multifirm environmental problem solving because of the perceived connections in the value chain: "You need all actors in the chain to successfully implement environmental innovations" (p. 176). The development of new sustainable technology and the awareness of the importance of cooperation across organizational and industrial boundaries make clear the need for "cradle-to-cradle" design. In cradle-to-cradle design, according to one of the interviewees, "all materials that are used to produce a product are reused in a second production process, and so on; in an ongoing cycle of use and reuse" (p. 157). Besides the technical aspect of design for sustainability, the organizational aspect can be distinguished. Designers may also need to consider the organizational aspects of their designs and their effects on sustainability. They can, for example, select suppliers of production materials that are located near the firm and not at the other side of the world. This can reduce transportation costs and emissions. With respect to this, an interviewee says that his firm "looks at economic and technical constraints. We build and analyze a business case before we start. We ask ourselves questions like: Do we minimize transportation? Can we sell residual heat to an organization nearby? Where do we have to locate our production facilities to optimize our economical and sustainable performance?" (p. 161). Many parameters can be taken into account when a design-for-sustainability approach is broadened with nontechnical parameters such as organizational and social factors. Companies can, for example, develop and design products and services and choose what position to aim for in market and society. As one of the respondents says: "Companies can be very reactive, minimize their efforts and comply with environmental legislation. Some firms do more than that, also have a dynamic environmental management system, and develop their own take on sustainability . . . and some firms even want to be the best sustainably innovative company of the nation, be a real frontrunner" (p. 222).

10.5   DEEPENING THE THEORETICAL BASIS

The review of the literature further reveals that knowledge and technology can be major factors at the co-institutionalization level of eco-innovative and sustainable practice in industry.

Brady and Davies (2004) establish that some innovative firms apply so-called business-led learning practices and routines to learn from their innovation projects and capture knowledge for the long run. They state that it is important that "the project-led learning processes are embedded within the wider business organization and strategic context of the firm" (p. 1608). A firm's technology leadership is often a strategic process in which a firm strategically chooses what it wants to learn from its innovation projects and, on the basis of the lessons learnt in these projects, develops new routinized processes and installs renewed or completely new business processes. Operational elements of such business-led learning are the creation of new divisions in the organization where the new innovative business can grow and a refocus of the core activities of the organization. Brady and Davis's (2004) view is that the capturing of knowledge from innovation projects and the use of this knowledge to redesign the company can add innovative power to the firm. Brady and Davis (2004) stress the importance of knowledge and technology. One of their main messages is that it is important not only to develop new knowledge in a co-innovative practice but also to integrate it into the firm and to try to make it part of the firm's standardized business processes and commercial activities.

Research also stresses the importance of using visualization (Cacciatori, 2008; Whyte, Ewenstein, Hales and Tidd, 2008) and codification practices (Boh, 2007; Cacciatori, 2008; Prencipe and Tell, 2001) to improve the tangibility, applicability and transferability of the knowledge that is developed in innovation projects and that is to be reused in other contexts. According to Whyte, Ewenstein, Hales and Tidd (2008), visualization techniques can be used to direct projects that explore new fields of interest and projects that aim to exploit new knowledge, techniques, products and processes for the firm. Visualization contributes to the "effectiveness at sense-making by making the outcomes of . . . work and the interfaces between them more visible and available for discussion among the team" (p. 87). In addition to being visualized through a graphical representation, knowledge can also be codified in work procedures, product and process specifications and in databases (Boh, 2007; Cacciatori, 2008; Prencipe and Tell, 2001). Information technology can support this codification, and, according to Boh (2007), information can be "carefully codified and stored in databases and documents, where it can be accessed and used easily by employees in the company" (p. 30). Operational elements of visualization and codification of knowledge are the use of visual materials such as charts, roadmaps, timelines, three-dimensional drawings, plans and photographs (Cacciatori, 2008; Prencipe and Tell, 2001; Whyte, Ewenstein, Hales and Tidd, 2008) and the use of computer-aided design (CAD) software (Whyte, Ewenstein, Hales and Tidd, 2008) and networked computers with procedures, roadmaps and databases (Boh, 2007; Prencipe and Tell, 2001). This visualization and codification of knowledge can support companies in capturing knowledge and technology and can add to their technological capabilities. Many technologies originate from people's desire to apply knowledge and create something. Knowledge is often tacit and intangible. By being captured in designs, drawings or texts, knowledge becomes formalized.

A specific technology that is frequently used to create sustainable product designs is the sustainable-design tool. The sustainable design is often based on life-cycle analysis (LCA) (see also Appendix 5). Innovative commercial firms in industry can apply sustainable-design tools that enable them to choose and evaluate sustainable materials, energy options and design alternatives (see also Appendix 6). Most design tools are based on life-cycle assessments (LCAs) of products and installations (Manfredi, Pant, Pennington and Versmann, 2011). The LCA qualifies and quantifies all environmental effects arising from the production, use and disposal of a material or product. The design tools offer sustainable alternatives for traditional and unsustainable design options. Most design tools quantify and qualify the positive and negative environmental effects of the application of materials, energy supply and production methods. Aspects of environmental friendliness that are qualified and quantified in a sustainable-design tool are, for example, depletion of natural resources, deforestation, acid rain, greenhouse emissions, recyclability, toxicity and biodiversity.

Finally, an administrative instrument that is used by companies to redesign business processes and integrate sustainability in their business processes is the environmental management system or corporate social responsibility policy. According to Donnelly, Olds, Blechinger, Reynolds and Beckett-Furnell (2004), the International Standardization Organization (ISO) 14000 series of standards can useful for this purpose (see Appendices 2–6). The ISO 14000 norm series provides organizational guidelines to integrate sustainability into product-design processes and to develop products with reduced environmental impact, lower greenhouse gas emissions, fewer ozone-depleting substances and reduced smog potential. The standard provides guidelines to improve a product's sustainable performance during its life cycle. Donnelly, Olds, Blechinger, Reynolds and Beckett-Furnell (2004) substantiate that all products from a firm need so-called change management, which means that, from time to time, products should be adjusted, get new features, be produced in another production plant or be marketed differently. For all these changes, also, environmental impact can be assessed and improved. The ISO 14000 norm series can be of assistance here. For example, it provides guidelines for the reuse and recycling of products that normally end up as waste. The norm series also prescribes how external auditors and internal auditors can be asked to review the sustainable-product-design processes, production processes and materials-handling and usage processes of the firm. It prescribes how firms can learn from reviewers' comments and further improve their system for environmental care. The ISO 14000 norm series is an organizational instrument that can add to design for sustainability.

The research in this chapter indicates that knowledge and technology can be powerful dynamic forces and drivers behind the institutionalization of sustainable innovation in industry. Knowledge flow and technological drive can put pressure on and provide incentives for firms to generate substantive

Table 10.1 Frame of Reference for Knowledge and Technology's Influence on Eco- and Sustainable Innovation in Industry

Knowledge and technology	Characteristics
Knowledge flow	Knowledge flow is a basic element of innovation dynamics in firms and between firms, is a basic element of innovation dynamics in industry and between industries, comes from geographic knowledge concentrations such as science parks, science cities and innovation regions, needs to be facilitated by firms by enabling employees to network with people inside and outside the firm, needs codification and visualization techniques to capture knowledge.
Technological drive	Technological drive enables firms to sustainably innovate, creates technology-demanding customers and markets, enables firms to operate a technology strategy, enables firms with a (re)combination strategy to continuously innovate.
Design for sustainability	Design for sustainability creates the eco-innovative and sustainable products of the future, integrates eco-innovation and sustainability in the structure of products, integrates eco-innovation and sustainability in the firm's production processes, exceeds organizational boundaries and concentrates on interorganizational value in the supply-production-consumption-reuse chain, uses design tools that are based on LCAs and ISO norms.

sustainable business. The frame of reference in Table 10.1 shows the characteristics of knowledge and technology that can drive eco- and sustainable innovation.

The research in this chapter indicates that knowledge and technology can stimulate organizations to grow their eco- and sustainably innovative businesses toward mass production and consumption.

10.6 SUMMARY

Knowledge and technology are the second element at the co-institutionalization level of the model of eco-innovation and sustainability. The research shows that knowledge exchange and technological development can enable firms to adopt a sustainable technology leadership strategy and become sustainable innovators. By combining and recombining already available technologies with new sustainable technologies, firms can conquer the market and can outperform competitors. Highly innovative firms can rely on their capacity to absorb and apply the latest knowledge and to facilitate and stimulate their workforce to interact with experts and people from other departments, organizations and industries. This can add to firms' capacity to integrate eco- and sustainable knowledge and technology into their designs for new products and models for new businesses. Knowledge and technology are important institutional factors that enable sustainably innovating firms to grow large, conquer the market and change industry, and they are the second factor at the co-institutionalization level. The third and last important factor at the co-institutionalization level is policy and regulation, which is the subject of the next chapter.

11 Co-institutionalization by Policy and Regulation

11.1 INTRODUCTION

The third category of factors at the co-institutionalization level is the category of policy and regulation. Policy and regulation can support and stimulate a nation's transformation from an unsustainable into a sustainable version of industry and society. A nation's policy and regulatory framework can show in what direction the nation should develop. It can describe and prescribe for the nation what is allowed, what is prohibited and what kind of business can be preferred for a more sustainable society. National policy and regulation thus can direct the future development of a nation. It can allocate public funding and decide what eco-innovative initiatives will be supported financially. It can state what the government and the governmental organizations will do in the next years to sustain the inhabitability of the country. It can describe what will be done in the fields of social security, preservation and development of natural resources and can anticipate demographic developments in the country. Public policy and regulation are primary a responsibility of governmental organizations, but these organizations need cooperation from commercial firms that put some policy into practice and comply with regulation. Often the governmental departments and organizations develop action programs, plans and projects to implement policy and regulative schemes and try to commit incumbent firms and small and medium-sized enterprises (SMEs) to the implementation of these policies and regulations. In a cooperative process, the nation's policy and regulation can be translated into activities that have to be undertaken by both public and private organizations. Policy and regulation can stimulate and force organizations to grow their eco- and sustainably innovative businesses toward mass production and consumption. Policy and regulation are the third element at the co-institutionalization level of the model of eco-innovation and sustainability management (see Figure 11.1).

This chapter first organizes the theory that forms the basis of the policy and regulation element of the model (Section 11.2). It describes the methods that are used to explore the analytical validity of this element for industry (Section 11.3). Then it explores the analytical value of this element in

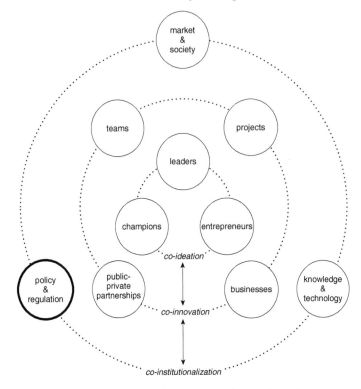

Figure 11.1   Co-institutionalization by policy and regulation.

practice (Section 11.4) and in theory (Section 11.5). It concludes with a summary (Section 11.6).

11.2   THEORETICAL BASIS

Government, industry and society are confronted with the challenge of integrating sustainable issues into their national policies, production systems and consumption patterns. A nation's transformation toward sustainability can be defined as the coherent and coordinated set of governmental, industrial and societal contributions to a "process of change in which the exploitation of resources, the direction of investments, the orientation of technological development, and institutional change are made consistent with future as well as present needs" (Brundtland and Khalid, 1987). Important questions that are related to the road to sustainable environmental development and sustained quality of life include these: How can environmental issues be integrated into national policy and regulation, and how can national environmental policy and regulation be implemented in a nation's public governance and industrial activity? Previous research suggests that cooperation among governmental, institutional, scientific and commercial organizations can facilitate environmental activity in existing networks of established organizations and in emerging networks of relatively young organizations (Chiffoleau, 2005; Smith, Stirling and Berkhout, 2005; Tsoutsos and Stamboulis, 2005). It also indicates that a national policy and a regulation scheme can stimulate organizations' sustainably conscious performance and can define a situation in which public and private organizations cooperatively develop and execute environmental action plans (Dewick and Miozzo, 2004; Kivimaa and Mickwitz, 2006).

Policy Planning

Kivimaa and Mickwitz (2006) propose that the state of the environment can be directed to a significant degree by a system of national policy planning. Policy strategies are used to direct governmental activities toward sustainability. On the level of policy strategies, representatives of the government, national institutions, research centers and commercial firms strategically review the nation's sustainability policies of the past. The insights that result from the reviews can be used to develop a new national sustainability strategy for the future. The starting point is that dissatisfaction with the current environmental state can induce policy pressure that stimulates or forces organizations to change and preserve environmental conditions (Kivimaa and Mickwitz, 2006). The underlying concept is that the environment can be controlled, changed and improved by human force. Gladwin, Kennelly and Krause (1995) support this point of view and argue that the awareness of human responsibility and the human connection to nature can be directed toward the development of technology that improves the quality of the environment and life. In addition to this, according to King (1995), the process of environmental innovation can be initiated and controlled by institutional organizations. Because ecological problems are often caused by individualism and self-interest, a nation may need national policy to protect common interests such as the state of the environment, life conditions and social relations.

Action Programs

Action programs can be used to develop initiatives that fit with the chosen policy strategies. According to Kivimaa and Mickwitz (2006), national action programs can be defined and selected by top governmental, institutional, scientific and firm representatives. The national action programs can consist of several technology programs, and all these programs can include a set of environmental objectives. Other sources in the literature also proclaim that policy pressure to preserve or change the environment has to be translated into action programs. Sigurdson and Cheng (2001), for example, argue that a national innovation policy enables research, invention and development of the new technologies that are needed to transform a nation's production system. Kivimaa and Mickwitz (2006) argue that the national action programs can initiate activity on an operational level. At the operational level, applied innovation projects can be executed in which governmental, institutional, scientific and commercial organizations cooperate. Clark and Paolucci (2001) have a similar message and argue that the funding of innovation projects that aim to develop innovative sustainable technology can be a significant factor in an environmentally aware industry and society. In line with this, Chiffoleau (2005), Smith, Stirling and Berkhout (2005) and Tsoutsos and Stamboulis (2005) establish that the transition of a nation's industries toward sustainability can depend on cooperation between public and private organizations and on their efforts to transform traditional products and processes into environmentally conscious ones.

Regulatory Assurance

Legislation can also be a key element of regulatory assurance. In most countries, the government has the legal right to impose restrictions on governmental and commercial organizations. The basic concept here is that governments can establish codes of conduct and levels of performance and that the nation's authorities and private organizations have to work within the boundaries of these rules (Brío and Junquera, 2003; Nameroff, Garant and Albert, 2004). Most countries have general laws that can be used to set new or additional sustainability requirements. Many countries, for example, already have legislation on air pollution, noise, soil protection and waste management. By tightening the requirements of these laws, countries can quickly and effectively ensure that limits on pollution are protected. This method is intended mainly for companies that do not want or are not able to cooperate and that refuse to implement the changes. The government "solves" this by standardizing and prescribing sustainability measures that have proved to be applicable in practice, for example in public-private demonstrations. A general conclusion that is supported by research is that regulation often tends to rely mainly on coercion and often does not stimulate spontaneous sustainable behavior by actors in the field (Cetindamar, 2003; Rothwell, 1992). Spontaneous sustainable behavior often comes from other sources, such as companies' or individuals' intrinsic ambitions and motivations. Gann, Wang and Hawkins (1998), for example, studied the effects of regulation on the innovativeness of the construction industry in the United Kingdom. They find that prescriptive regulation actually stifles firms' creativity. In addition to this, their research shows that performance-based regulation—that is, regulation that stimulates organizations to innovate in a certain direction without strict norms and measures—can be far more effective and can challenge firms to develop their own innovative solutions and approaches.

11.3   RESEARCH METHOD

Additional empirical and theoretical studies are performed to further increase the analytical value of the policy and regulation element of the model of eco-innovation and sustainability management for industry.

Step 1.   Shaping the Research Model

This chapter builds on the results from the initial study of Bossink (2011a) (see Appendix 1). It focuses on the policy and regulation element of the model (Section 11.2). It conducts empirical research in the Dutch trade industry to study how the policy and regulation element of the model holds for another empirical context (Section 11.4). It carries out a literature review of the influence of policy and regulation on the sustainability of industry in order to explore how this element of the model can be shaped toward a broader analytical value for industry (Section 11.5).

Step 2.   Conducting Theoretical and Empirical Studies

Literature databases are consulted for research papers that deal with the influence of policy and regulation on environmental, ecological, green, social, societal, biological and sustainably innovative initiatives in industry. In addition, ten managers and experts in the Dutch trade industry are interviewed and are asked to reflect on the influence of policy and regulation on sustainability issues in their industry (Roeloffzen, 2010).

Step 3.   Analyzing and Synthesizing the Studies' Outcomes

The policy and regulation element in the initial model (Bossink, 2011a) is confronted with the additional empirical and theoretical studies. On the basis of the outcomes of this analysis, the characteristics of the policy and regulation element at the co-institutionalization level are articulated for industry (Section 11.5).

11.4   EXPLORING THE EMPIRICAL FIELD

The exploratory interviews confirm that policy and regulation can stimulate an industry's eco-innovative and sustainable capability. Respondents agree that cooperation between public and private organizations is a condition for the fruitful realization of national sustainable policy plans. Regulation is also seen as an important instrument to institutionalize standards for sustainability and eco-innovation. This section is the author's interpretation of Roeloffzen (2010), and quotations are taken from that source.

Policy Planning

A majority of the respondents state that they are fully aware of the government's responsibility. They know that the government has primary responsibility for protecting and improving common goods, including the country's social arrangements, its societal structures, the distribution of public property and human rights, personal safety and well-being, environmental conditions, and the inhabitability of the country. This implies that the government needs to develop national policy with regard to social, societal and environmental issues and has to develop a vision for the future state of the country. Respondents are also aware that the government by itself is not capable of realizing most of the goals that are set in its policy plans. It needs cooperation and initiatives from companies and nongovernmental organizations. According to several respondents, this is a rather difficult aspect of a nation's sustainable policy planning process. It is often problematic to commit companies to sustainable policy planning, because too often companies still think in terms of classic economic mechanisms. The most important goal in this classical approach is to realize growth, to increase turnovers and to maximize financial profit. A respondent of a commercial company, for example, puts it as follows: "Forty percent of the government's environmental goals will not be realized because we—companies—do not cooperate. We can only think about economic growth. We are in denial. Lack of sustainable practice is not a problem to us. . . . Enterprises are too much focused on generating growth and making a profit. When that is the main focus of an organization, environmental conditions remain underexposed" (p. 41). Most respondents touch upon the necessity of cooperation among firms and agree that a lot of progress can be made with respect to this issue. They, for example, state that there is a "chain of responsibility" and that this chain consists of governmental, nongovernmental and commercial organizations. This implies not only that the government has a primary responsibility for a nation's sustainable policy planning but also that nongovernmental and commercial organizations have a responsibility to join the process of national sustainable policy planning. The respondents say that firms have the obligation to support the government and to cooperate with the authorities to implement sustainable policy in practice. Interviewees recognize that this can be advantageous, even in terms of financial profitability and companies' turnover. When society is transforming toward sustainability, it can be a plus for a firm to have experience with sustainable business. Experience can provide a company a competitive advantage in the marketplace. A respondent, for example, remarks that his firm has experience with sustainable business and therefore has "a knowledge-based advantage. We know the risks and opportunities" (p. 47), and this enables his company to stay one step or even more steps ahead of the competition. Another respondent turns it around and says: "I think that when you do not implement a sustainability policy, you can have a competitive disadvantage" (p. 47).

Action Programs

While most governmental organizations use their resources to develop national and regional policy and offer public services to the people, industry concentrates on mass production and delivery of commercial products and services. The Dutch government has no or little physical production capacity or market-based commercial interests, and it depends on industry when it comes to realizing policy in practice. When policy plans have been made by the authorities, an important next step then can be to define action programs to be carried out by public private consortia, partnerships and alliances. Although the state can have influence on these forms of cooperation through subsidy programs, assigning of penalties and provision of knowledge support, the commercial firms are in the driver's seat. Their willingness and commitment can determine whether an eco-innovative action, project or program will succeed or fail. The interviews indicate that most companies are not eager to take a risk. Only a small number of enterprises dare to invest in sustainability, believe in growing market shares for sustainable business, and join the government in the action programs. In practice, it often appears that a so-called small world of firms and people commits itself to the governmental action plans. This means that a small, invariable group of people and firms cooperate with the government in all plans, all the time, while the large majority of people and firms are absent and not committed to the national sustainable action plans. One of the respondents, for example, remarks that it always is the same group of companies that participates and adds that "the meetings with [the governmental client] and other organizations involved are becoming a déjà vu . . . it becomes a small circle with sustainable experts" (p. 38). This small world of governmental, nongovernmental and commercial organizations meets and cooperates to implement the action plans and, while doing this, discovers that sustainable business can become profitable. A respondent from a large company remarks that " 'sustainability' is also 'doing business.' If we work more efficiently with materials, it will cut costs. When [my firm] is capable of reducing CO_2 emissions our production costs will go down substantially" (p. 49). Various interviewees think that, because the government has primary responsibility and at the same time depends on industry for its success, it should invest in cooperation with industry. It can, for example, offer additional financial resources to companies that are willing to cooperate. The interviewees also mention that the authorities can offer knowledge by creating knowledge centers and by being the national coordination center for all public-private initiatives, demonstrations, experiments and pilot studies. Such an organizational structure can give firms access to knowledge and to examples of next practices.

Regulatory Assurance

The interviewees' companies struggle with sustainable regulation. They are confronted with regulation that changes each year, and it is difficult to develop new routines when the speed of regulatory change is that fast. In addition, the interviewees remark that it is hard to interpret environmental regulation. Regulatory measures often consist of many criteria and weightings. The reasons for the selection of these criteria and weightings are not always clear; they are sometimes subjective and, on top of that, are subject to change. This confuses companies, which often do not have the time, competence and commitment to delve into the details of regulation. In addition, compliance with LCA-based regulation is complicated, and firms find it a complex business to, for example, improve the energy efficiency of their production sites and products. Respondents indicate that there is a need for a thoroughly developed and standardized measurement instrument that is made part of national regulation and that is improved or changed on a regular basis. They think that at this moment there are too many different measurement instruments and that it is unclear what the basic or main standard is for regulation.

11.5   DEEPENING THE THEORETICAL BASIS

The review of the literature indicates that both government and industry have a prominent position and function in effective national innovation policy and regulation.

According to Sigurdson and Cheng (2001), both national and corporate innovation policies have to support industry in institutionalizing innovation. It is their view that the nation's innovation policy is made by the government as well as by commercial companies. This means that industrial development is directed by governmental and corporate policy. The nation's governmental organizations develop national innovation policies, and this can lead to research, invention, development and adoption of new technology. Sigurdson and Cheng (2001) contend that governmental policy has the potential to set an R&D agenda for science and business. In many countries, such an R&D agenda is effectuated by a system in which government-related organizations evaluate and fund research proposals from scholars from universities, independent research laboratories and high-tech start-up firms. Sigurdson and Cheng (2001) establish that governmentally induced R&D can be complemented by industrial, firm-owned policy for R&D and innovation. Firms can develop their own autonomous corporate innovation policies. This implies that firms do not just wait for the government to decide where the country is heading but also develop their own R&D vision and innovation strategy for future business and tomorrow's competitive position. Most firms are aware of the importance of R&D and innovative activity and integrate a technology and innovation policy into their corporate strategies. This gives direction to their activities, which focus on inventions, development of new products and services and the adoption of new technologies. Sigurdson and Cheng (2001) emphasize that both types of policy—governmental policy and corporate policy—can stimulate the innovativeness of the nation's industries.

According to Bossink (2002a, 2011a), regulation can be derived from next practices that are developed by public-private partnerships. Next-practice-based regulation can be used to force lagging companies and innovation-averse firms to adopt a minimum level of innovation that has been developed by the innovators in industry. Highly innovative firms are often strategically committed to participation in public-private partnerships through which they can benefit from governmental incentives and learn to innovate in a new societal direction. Many innovations can be developed and tested in national public-private partnerships. Often, the innovative knowledge is rather "sticky." It becomes part of the skill set and capabilities of the professionals and firms that cooperate in the public-private partnership and tends to stay there without diffusing to other firms in the country that did not join the public-private partnerships. New innovative knowledge thus can be owned by a small group of firms and people. The tendency of knowledge to remain within a small world of a just few people and firms has many potential causes. Participants in public-private partnerships, for example, may see their repeated and exclusive participation as an important means to sustain and strengthen their business. It can deepen their ability to develop environmentally sustainable innovations and can strengthen their position as specialists in the business landscape. Another reason for this lock-in of knowledge can be that further advancement of innovative solutions becomes more important to participants in public-private partnerships than finding ways to apply fragments of next practices in other settings. Participants in public-private partnerships can form inward-oriented networks that focus on the development of sophisticated resources and capabilities without paying attention to knowledge exchanges with other organizations in industry. In addition, firms that do not join a public-private partnership may choose to remain in their comfort zone and want to continue to work in a traditional way, the way that they are used to. Even when public-private partnerships open their knowledge portfolios and aim to share new knowledge, these firms may not want to have it, do not need it and prefer to stay ignorant. Another cause of the lack of diffusion of knowledge from public-private partnerships to firms in industry can be that the knowledge is difficult to transfer, because of so-called learning boundaries, a concept coined by Scarbrough, Swan, Laurent, Bresnen, Edelman and Newell (2004). They define learning boundaries as "the boundaries to the transfer of learning between projects and other organizational units" (p. 1580). Learning boundaries tend to constrain the exploitation of the benefits of project-led learning for the wider organization. The difficulty of transferring what is learned from a project to other contexts can be caused by the absence of organizational communities of people who appropriate the knowledge and practices of the project-based communities. Most firms often also do not have the right organizational means, such as procedures, norms and behavioral

Table 11.1   Frame of Reference for Policy and Regulation's Influence on Eco- and Sustainable Innovation in Industry

Policy and regulation	Characteristics
Policy planning	National policy induces a nation's sustainable development, is a primary responsibility of the government, highly depends for its success on collaboration with industry, directs government's and firms' sustainable activity.
Action programs	Action programs are derived from governmental policy plans, have to be aligned with firms' corporate strategies, consist of applied public-private projects in which governmental and nongovernmental organizations, universities and industry cooperate.
Regulatory assurance	Regulatory assurance enables the introduction of sustainability standards for society and industry, puts pressure on lagging organizations to innovate and comply with minimum innovation standards.

codes, to accumulate and appropriate project-based learning experience. In addition to this, Scarbrough, Swan, Laurent, Bresnen, Edelman and Newell (2004) argue that "most learning in projects is based on knowledge integration activities, which involve overcoming, rather than deepening, divisions of practice among project members," while most "mainstream and routinized work practices . . . are conducive to . . . specialization and evolving communities of practice" (p. 1585). Scarbrough, Swan, Laurent, Bresnen, Edelman and Newell (2004) emphasize this by stating that "the corollary here is that the greater the degree of learning within the project, the greater the division between the new, shared practices of project members and the practices obtaining in other parts of the organization" (p. 1585). Limited knowledge diffusion from public-private partnerships to other organizational forms indicates that it can be necessary for regulation to stimulate and force less innovative firms to appropriate some of the new knowledge on sustainability that is available from the next practices that are developed by public-private partnerships.

The research in this chapter indicates that policy and regulation can be important drivers of the institutionalization of eco- and sustainable innovation in industry. Policy plans, action plans and regulatory arrangements can put pressure on and can provide incentives for firms to generate substantive sustainable businesses. The frame of reference in Table 11.1 shows the characteristics of policy and regulation that potentially drive eco- and sustainable innovation in industry.

The research in this chapter indicates that policy and regulation can stimulate organizations to grow their eco- and sustainably innovative businesses toward mass production and consumption.

11.6   SUMMARY

Policy and regulation are the third element at the co-institutionalization level of the model of eco-innovation and sustainability. The research shows that policy and regulation can be necessary to start and ensure the sustainable innovation process in industry. Policy can be needed to provide a general level of innovative ambition for the country and to allocate public resources to national innovation programs and initiatives. Successful policy can be policy in which the authorities, universities, nongovernmental organizations and commercial industry cooperate. Despite this, there are often also companies that do not cooperate and that choose to stick to traditional and unsustainable practices. With respect to this, regulation can be needed to ensure that a certain minimum level of eco- and sustainable innovation becomes standardized and obligatory to all organizations in industry. Policy and regulation are the third and final element at the co-institutionalization level of the model. Now that the model is complete and all elements at all three levels of the model have been presented, the model can be discussed as a whole. This is the subject of the next and final chapter.

12 Eco-innovation and Sustainability Management

12.1 INTRODUCTION

This final chapter provides a concise recapitulation of the model of eco-innovation and sustainability management (Section 12.2). It describes the major roles that can be performed by professionals who want to contribute to eco-innovation and sustainability in practice (Section 12.3), and it addresses these professionals' main challenges and business opportunities (Section 12.4). This final chapter ends with the major limitations of the model of eco-innovation and sustainability and provides several avenues for further research (Section 12.5).

12.2 MODEL OF ECO-INNOVATION AND SUSTAINABILITY MANAGEMENT

This section aims to recapitulate the essentials of the model of eco-innovation and sustainability management for industry. Detailed descriptions and discussions of the model's elements are included in the previous chapters. The model's central point of view is that eco- and sustainable innovation can be conceptualized as a system that consists of three interdependent and interacting levels of cooperative activity (see Figure 12.1).

Three dotted circles symbolize the three managerial levels of the eco- and sustainable innovation system. The dotted circle in the center represents the co-ideation level. The surrounding dotted circle visualizes the co-innovation level. The outer dotted circle symbolizes the co-institutionalization level. The double-headed arrows between these dotted circles visualize the linear, cyclic and interactive interactions between these levels. The balls, situated on the dotted circles, represent the elements at each level. The co-ideation level consists of leaders, champions and entrepreneurs. The co-innovation level consists of teams, projects, businesses and public-private partnerships. The co-institutionalization level consists of market and society, knowledge and technology, and policy and regulation. The co-ideation level of the model comprises the people in firms who take the lead, see market opportunities,

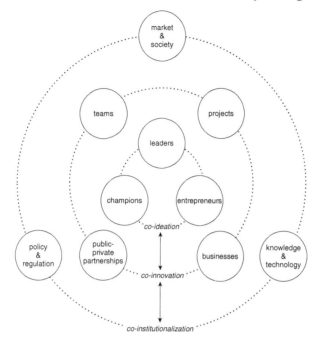

Figure 12.1   The eco-innovation and sustainability management system.

dare to come with creative ideas and want their organizations to become environmental and sustainable innovators. These people have a central position in the eco-innovation and sustainability model. The co-innovation level of the model concentrates on the organizational forms in which these key individuals cooperate and transform some of their ideas into real business propositions that generate market share. The co-institutionalization level of the model focuses on the business environmental factors that enable these new business proposals to grow large and to become the new eco-innovative and sustainable standards in industry and society. The main claims of the model of eco-innovation and sustainability are that eco- and sustainable innovation is (a) created by cooperating individuals (e.g., leaders, entrepreneurs and champions) in (b) networks of various organizational forms (e.g., teams, projects, businesses and public-private partnerships) and (c) is facilitated to grow into substantive business by several institutional factors (e.g., market and society, knowledge and technology, and policy and regulation).

12.3   ROLES, GOALS AND MEASURES IN THE SYSTEM

This section describes the major roles that can be performed by professionals who want to contribute to eco-innovation and sustainability in practice.

Table 12.1   Managerial Roles, Goals and Measures in the System

Level and element	Role	Goal (and measure)
Co-ideation	Being a(n):	Generate sustainable ideas:
Leaders	Leader	with societal impact (# stakeholder-serving ideas)
Entrepreneurs	Entrepreneur	that generate new business (# business ideas)
Champions	Champion	that create new products/ services (# product/service ideas)
Co-innovation	Being a:	Develop sustainable innovations:
Teams	Team player	across organizational boundaries (# (in)formal innovation teams)
Projects	Project member	within cost and time constraints (# innovation projects)
Businesses	Business(wo)man	that deliver turnover and profit (# turnover/profit)
Public-private partnerships	P-P partner	that have growth potential (% turnover/profit growth)
Co-institutionalization	Being a:	Institutionalize sustainable innovations by:
Market and society	Marketer	selling their added value to customers (# publicity campaigns)
Knowledge and technology	Knowledge worker	means of cross-boundary production chains (# joint ventures)
Policy and regulation	Game changer	means of standardized incentives and force (# funding and rules)

In the system of eco-innovation and sustainability people can play different roles and can have unique contributions to innovation in their own organization and in the innovation system as a whole. Table 12.1 gives an overview of the roles that innovative people can perform at the three levels of the sustainable innovation system (see the first two columns). Table 12.1 lists the major goal for each role and a key measure that can be used to direct and evaluate a person's performance of this role (see the third column). The roles, goals and measures are based on the model and on the characteristics of the model's elements.

Co-ideation

Leaders

The eco-innovative and sustainable leader's goal is to generate sustainable ideas that have an impact on society. The leader's sustainable innovativeness can be measured by counting and evaluating his or her stakeholder-serving ideas. A sustainable leader, for example, can address the firm's opportunities with respect to cleaner production, reuse of resources and serving shareholders and stakeholders. The eco-innovative and sustainable leader is dedicated to corporate social responsibility and sustainability and aims to develop a firm that contributes to societal value in a broader sense than just shareholder value.

Entrepreneurs

The eco-innovative and sustainable entrepreneur knows that sustainability can be important but also that economic targets have to be met. The eco-innovative and sustainable entrepreneur's goal is to generate ideas for new business. The entrepreneur's sustainable innovativeness can be measured by counting and evaluating the sustainable business ideas he or she produces. The entrepreneur is not overwhelmed by environmental problems such as the greenhouse effect. On the contrary, the entrepreneur sees these problems as an opportunity to generate new sustainable business. The entrepreneur aims to develop eco-innovative and sustainable business ideas that have potential in terms of turnovers and profits. The sustainable entrepreneur is not purely idealistic and wants to combine profitability and sustainability.

Champions

The eco-innovative and sustainable champion is the person who comes up with solutions and shows others what needs to be done to sustainably renew the company's processes, services and products. The eco-innovative and sustainable champion's goal is to create ideas for new sustainable products, services and business processes. The champion's sustainable innovativeness can be measured by counting and evaluating the ideas he or she generates to improve, renew or innovate products, services and business processes. The champion has a passion for the inventive part of ideation and wants to contribute to the future sustainable product and service portfolio of the company.

Co-innovation

Team Players

Eco-innovative and sustainable teams need loyal team players. The eco-innovative and sustainable team player's goal is to contribute to the transformation of innovative ideas into sustainable business. The team player knows that eco- and sustainable innovation requires teamwork from people from different departments and locations and that team members have to cross departmental and organizational boundaries. A team player's sustainably innovative activity can be measured by counting and evaluating the business proposals that are developed by the (in)formal innovation teams he or she joins. Many persons in a company are not in a position to be the leader or do not have the drive, knowledge or character to be the entrepreneur or the champion of sustainable innovation. These people have the possibility to be loyal team players who cooperate with leaders, entrepreneurs and champions and become part of the innovative process.

Project Members

Eco-innovative and sustainable projects need committed project members. The eco-innovative and sustainable project member's goal is to contribute to the transformation of innovative ideas into sustainable business by managing, coordinating and contributing to innovation projects and to develop and deliver the desired innovations within cost and time constraints. A project member's sustainably innovative activity can be measured by counting and evaluating the business proposals that are developed by the innovation projects he or she joins. Eco-innovative and sustainable project members contribute to the transformation of innovative ideas into emerging businesses.

Business(wo)men

Eco-innovative and sustainable businesses need active business(wo)men. Eco-innovative and sustainable business(wo)men's goal is to contribute to the transformation of innovative ideas into sustainable business by generating sustainable initiatives that have sufficient turnover and that generate considerable financial profits. Their contribution to sustainable innovation can be measured by counting and evaluating the turnovers and profits the firm generates through the business(wo)men's newly introduced sustainable businesses. Eco-innovative and sustainable business(wo)men know that sustainable business transcends the boundaries of departments, organizations and even industrial sectors. They thus concentrate on interfirm sustainable business generation.

Public-Private Partners

Eco-innovative and sustainable public-private partnerships need skilled public-private partners. The eco-innovative and sustainable public-private partner's goal is to contribute to the transformation of innovative ideas into sustainable business by generating innovative initiatives that are embedded in society and have the potential to grow and gain larger market shares. The public-private partner's contribution to sustainable innovation can be measured by considering and evaluating the percentage of turnover and profit growth an organization realizes through cooperation with governmental and nongovernmental organizations in public-private partnerships. Cooperating public and private actors work together because of a shared vision. They try to develop sustainable innovations that serve business and common interest and have the potential to become new nationwide standards.

Co-institutionalization

Marketers

Market and societal changes that institutionalize eco-innovation and sustainability need competent marketers. The marketer's goal is to contribute to the institutionalization of sustainable innovations by promoting and selling the new eco-innovative products and services to the customer. A measure of the marketer's contribution to institutionalization is the number and impact of his or her publicity campaigns for sustainable products and services. The marketer knows that people are willing to pay for quality and that sustainability can be positioned as an additional quality aspect. The marketer informs the customer about the superior sustainable quality of the new products and services.

Knowledge Workers

Knowledge and technology dynamics that institutionalize eco-innovation and sustainability need qualified knowledge workers. The knowledge worker's goal is to institutionalize sustainable innovations by contributing to the sustainability of the value chains in industry that often intersect organizational boundaries. A measure of the knowledge worker's contribution to the institutionalization of eco-innovation and sustainability is the number of joint ventures in which she or he participates and their quantitative and qualitative impact. An industry's sustainability level can be increased when knowledge workers cooperate across organizational boundaries and improve value chains on an interorganizational level.

Game Changers

New policy and regulation that institutionalize eco-innovation and sustainability need strategic game changers. The game changer's goal is to institutionalize sustainable innovations by contributing to the development and introduction of public policy and of regulation that is in favor of newly developed sustainable products and services. A measure of the game changer's contribution to institutionalization is to count and qualify the funding programs and rules, laws and procedures that the game changer introduces to enable sustainable firms to grow their business. Game changers know that policy and regulation can pave the way for new sustainable business and can support tiny sustainable businesses to become widely accepted and to grow large.

12.4 MANAGEMENT CHALLENGES
AND BUSINESS OPPORTUNITIES

This section addresses the major challenges and opportunities of eco-innovation and sustainability for professionals in practice. In the system of eco-innovation and sustainability, the people who play different roles all have their own managerial challenge and business opportunities. Table 12.2 presents these managerial challenges and business opportunities for all roles in the system. The management challenges and business opportunities are based on the model and the characteristics of the model's elements.

Co-ideation

The main management challenge for professionals at the co-ideation level is to integrate eco-innovation and sustainability into the corporate strategies of their firms. The related business opportunity is that their firms can gain the lead in new sustainability-oriented markets that can have a considerable growth potential. This implies that leaders, entrepreneurs and champions who strategically commit themselves to sustainability and who perceive sustainability as a value driver with the potential to generate income can have an advantage over competitors. Their prospect is to take the lead as an innovator. When markets for sustainability start to grow, their firms can

Table 12.2 Management Challenges and Business Opportunities

Level, element and role	Management challenge	Business opportunity
Co-ideation		
Leader	Integration of	Firms that lead in
Entrepreneur	sustainability in	new markets
Champion	corporate strategy	with growth
	of the firm	potential
Co-innovation		
Teams: Team player	Development of	Firms with a strong
Projects: Project member	sustainable and	long-term
Businesses: Business(wo)man	profitable	competitive
Public-private partnerships:	businesses	position
P-P partner		
Co-institutionalization		
Market and society: Marketer	Reinforcement of	Emergence of
Knowledge and technology:	demand for	sustainable
Knowledge worker	sustainability	industries and
Policy and regulation: Game		societies
changer		

have a first-mover advantage and a knowledge lead. They can leave behind competitors that have bet on unsustainable production. In addition, scarcity of resources, the hazards of toxicity and people's growing awareness that sustainability is important can further stimulate demand for eco-innovation and sustainability and lead to the ongoing growth of new markets that are completely oriented toward eco-innovation and sustainability. As co-creators of these markets, these professionals' firms have the opportunity to become the incumbents of the future.

Co-innovation

The main management challenge for team players, project members, business(wo)men and public-private partners at the co-innovation level is to develop businesses that are sustainable and profitable at the same time. The related business opportunity is that firms can develop a strong long-term competitive position in the market. Innovative sustainable business models can have the potential to push away the older and unsustainable business models. A sustainable business model serves multiple stakeholders. It thus has an increased potential to serve a large variety of groups in business and in society. Another advantage of a sustainable business model can be that it invests in creating value, that it includes quality aspects such as functionality, user friendliness and reliability but is not limited to this and includes ecological, social and societal specifications. This can extend the functionality and function of sustainable products and services to customers and clients and can result in an increased appeal to buyers and users. It can strengthen these professionals' firms' competitive position in markets.

Co-institutionalization

The main management challenge for marketers, knowledge workers and game changers at the co-institutionalization level is to further stimulate market and societal demand for sustainability. The related business opportunity is that when sustainability-oriented markets grow, new sustainable industries emerge. Technological development that focuses on the creation of new eco-innovations and sustainable solutions to problems can facilitate the growth of sustainable businesses. In addition, new policy and regulation that are in favor of eco-innovation and sustainability can improve the context in which eco-innovative firms do business and enable the emergence and growth of substantive new eco-innovative and sustainable businesses and markets.

12.5 LIMITATIONS AND DIRECTIONS FOR FURTHER RESEARCH

This final section concludes with the major limitations of the model of eco-innovation and sustainability and ends with important avenues for further research.

The three-level model of eco- and sustainable innovation management can have analytical value for various industrial settings. It can serve as a model and a frame of reference for studying, analyzing and improving industrial sustainable innovation systems. However, although the model is based on empirical research in Dutch building (Bossink, 2011a) and various other sectors of Dutch industry (this book) and is theoretically grounded in state-of-the-art theory of innovation and eco- and sustainable innovation (Bossink, 2011a and this book), its analytical value may also be limited. It can have analytical value for developed countries and for industries that are organized primarily according to modern standards in which democracy, justice, the economic principles of free markets, advanced industrial production systems and freedom of the people have reached a relatively high level of development. Not all countries and industries conform to these characteristics, and the model can have less analytical value for these other settings. Another limitation is that the model provides a basic structure of how and why eco-innovation and sustainability management in industry function. Nevertheless, it does not prescribe how eco-innovation and sustainability systems should function, nor does it predict how eco-innovation and sustainability systems will function in the future. The model is purely descriptive and does not have explicit explanatory or prescriptive value.

The model does imply that sustainable innovation at one of the three levels can and will be influenced by developments at another level and vice versa. The model focuses on a description and an exploration of the levels and their elements and on interactions among the levels and elements. It does not structurally delve into the possible reasons, mechanisms or attitudes that drive these interaction effects. Future research can focus on that. It can, for example, concentrate on the effects of governmental policy at the co-institutionalization level on the behavior of innovation leaders and champions at the co-ideation level. Or it can study the effects of public-private partnerships at the co-innovation level on the development of new eco-innovative regulation at the co-institutionalization level. Now that the basic levels and elements of the model are defined and described, future research needs to concentrate on a further in-depth analysis and explanation of interlevel and interelement interactions and interaction effects.

Appendices

Appendix 1
Main Conclusions from *Managing Environmentally Sustainable Innovation: Insights from the Construction Industry*

This book builds on empirical research by Bossink (2011a) in the Dutch construction industry. This appendix presents a selection of the main conclusions. This selection discusses innovation leadership, innovation championship, innovation team coordination, multiteam innovation projects, multiorganizational innovation projects, innovation drivers, innovation policy and international eco-issues.

INNOVATION LEADERSHIP

The research shows that leadership is needed to direct a sustainable innovation team toward an innovative ambition, goal and result. The leader can choose from a repertoire of different leadership styles. The performance of charismatic, instrumental, strategic and interactive innovation leadership has a stimulating effect on sustainable building innovation. A charismatic leadership style energizes team members and innovation champions to innovate and accelerates the sustainable innovation process. An instrumental leadership style structures and controls the sustainable innovation process of teams. A strategic leadership style uses hierarchical power to get teams to innovate in sustainability. The interactive leadership style empowers team members and champions to innovate and to become sustainable innovation leaders themselves.

INNOVATION CHAMPIONSHIP

The research findings also show that innovation champions are the creative source of innovative activity. It appears that the work of promoting, inventing, entrepreneurial and gatekeeping champions of innovation contributes to the sustainable innovation process in teams. A promoter endorses innovation by means of persuasion, lobbying and talking innovation. An inventor has the expertise to innovate and generates ideas, creativity and knowledge. An entrepreneur initiates innovation and stimulates new product and service development to open new markets and make money. The gatekeeper processes information about innovation, traces and shares knowledge and looks for trends.

INNOVATION TEAM COORDINATION

Furthermore, the research shows that several management styles can be performed to coordinate and control the innovation processes in a sustainable innovation team. To coordinate cooperation in innovation teams, a manager can use systems thinking, realistic creativity, innovation focus and process linking. A systems manager coordinates the innovation team as part of a larger whole and stresses interdependencies and exchanges with the business environment. A realistic-creative manager stimulates the innovation team's solutions that save or generate money, supports creative idea generation and selects creative ideas with market potential. A manager with an innovation focus emphasizes that everyone in the innovation team must be innovative, supports an innovative team culture and stresses possibilities for continuous innovation. A process-linking manager aligns the innovation team's output with the processes of the firm, has an overview of the organizational primary processes and seeks to connect team output with organizational processes. Simultaneous application of some but not necessarily all of these approaches successfully contributes to a productive sustainable innovation team. This means that a manager who fails to apply some of these approaches but masters the others has sufficient capabilities to successfully manage an effective sustainable innovation team.

MULTITEAM INNOVATION PROJECTS

The research shows that a varied set of management principles can be applied to coordinate and control the sustainably innovative activities of multiteam innovation projects. Management principles that stimulate sustainable innovation projects are design-driven, planning-oriented, systematic, targeted and positioning management. A design-driven manager makes his or her own innovation plans. Such a manager starts with a well-prepared project plan and sticks to the plan. A planning-oriented manager implements innovation step by step, starts with committing the participants to a collective schedule and focuses on agreements and monitoring progress. A systematic manager works with a logical view of innovation. This type of manager develops an integral view of the project and its business environment and directs the project completely by him- or herself. A targeting manager defines and realizes innovation goals, sets innovation goals that fit with the strategy of the firm and manages mainly for goal realization. A positioning manager uses innovation to gain a competitive advantage in the market, informing and listening to customers and using customer and user information to innovate. Simultaneous performance of some but not necessarily all management principles successfully contributes to the effectiveness of a sustainably innovative project.

MULTIORGANIZATIONAL INNOVATION PROJECTS

The research also shows that multiorganizational sustainable innovation projects go through several developmental stages of cooperative activity. It appears that organizations that consecutively go through all stages of the co-innovation process effectively develop sustainable projects with a high sustainability score. Co-innovating organizations and their managers go through nine stages. In the first stage, managers analyze the business environment and choose a certain innovative direction. In the second stage, managers explore the possibilities of co-innovating with others. In the third stage, managers negotiate about the resources each organization has to bring in. In the fourth stage, managers enter into contracts and agreements with others. In the fifth stage, they develop innovation plans with their partners. In the sixth stage, the managers establish a joint venture. In the seventh stage, the managers control the joint venture for individual and shared interests. In the eighth stage, they control the production of the innovations that are planned. Finally, in the ninth stage, they market and sell the innovations of the joint venture. Additionally, the research indicates that multiorganizational sustainable innovation projects often consist of cooperating governmental and commercial organizations. Managers who act in this playing field listen to and cooperate with the government. They follow the government's environmental plans, operate in accordance with legal requirements and rules and participate in financial incentives. Sustainably innovative managers also stimulate the use of sustainable design tools and of waste management practices. Managers who understand the public-private nature of sustainable business also join public-private partnerships. They participate in public-private agreements, demonstration projects and other R&D-oriented projects.

INNOVATION DRIVERS

The research shows that the business environment exercises considerable influence on organizations' sustainable activities. Business environmental factors that can become drivers of sustainable innovation projects are stakeholder pressure, technological capabilities and knowledge transfer. A manager who considers stakeholder pressure reviews the requests and demands from the business environment. This manager decides to respond to business force, to serve innovation-demanding customers and to act on governmental incentives, conditions and constraints. A manager who considers technological capabilities is open to the available technologies in the outside world and uses them where possible and needed, recombines existing parts into something new and implements a technology leadership strategy. A manager who considers knowledge transfer gets access to the necessary knowledge bases. This manager actively networks and encourages others to network for knowledge. He or she also exchanges information with many counterparts, partners, stakeholders and interest groups and stimulates cooperation across departmental and organizational boundaries. The research showed that simultaneous management attention to and action based on these innovation drivers contribute to the effectiveness of a sustainable innovation project.

INNOVATION POLICY

The government's sustainable policy also has an impact on the organizations in industry. The government's policy strategies plan the sustainable direction of the nation's industry for the longer term, and policy instruments translate these plans into programs that are supported and funded by the government and lead to certain outcomes. Managers who want to take advantage of the governmental environmental innovation policy join this process of national strategizing and participate in the public-private projects that originate from it.

INTERNATIONAL ISSUES

The international issues in sustainability that relate to building appear to be the change of substance cycles, depletion of raw materials, depletion of finite energy sources, climate change, acidification of atmosphere, drying of surface and loss of biodiversity. Public opinion encourages governments and firms to find solutions for these issues. A manager who wants to contribute, for example, can use products and services that slow down the change of substance cycles and secondary materials or infinite energy sources. A manager can also decide to use products and services that are carbon dioxide (CO_2), sulfur dioxide (SO_2), nitrogen oxide (NO_x) and ammonia (NH_3) neutral.

Appendix 2
ISO 14001 Environmental
Management Systems—Requirements
with Guidance for Use

The ISO 14001 standard provides the basic requirements of a firm's environmental management system (ISO, 2004a). In essence, it describes and prescribes a firm's environmental policy, procedures to put this policy into practice and the control and review activities to ensure the quality of these activities. Within this structure of policy planning, policy implementation and policy control and review, ISO 14001 aims to continually improve the management system in the company. The ISO 14001 standard provides the basics of what must be planned and must be done. Guidelines and examples of what to do more precisely can be found in ISO 14004 (see Appendix 3).

ISO 14001 gives guidelines, rules and requirements for several elements of a firm's management system for environmental care. These elements are general requirements, environmental policy, planning, implementation and operation, checking and management review.

GENERAL REQUIREMENTS

The firm must actively plan and specify its environmental performance.

ENVIRONMENTAL POLICY

The firm's top management has to describe and prescribe the firm's environmental policy. The firm's environmental policy defines what the firm will do to prevent pollution and what it will do to improve its pollution-prevention system. It states how the firm will comply with legal and social environmental requirements. Furthermore, it describes how the firm defines and accomplishes environmental goals and how the process of goal definition and achievement is documented. The environmental policy states how the firm communicates about the functioning of its environmental management system with personnel and other stakeholders.

PLANNING

The firm must have organizational procedures to identify, measure and document the environmental aspects of its business activities. These procedures ensure that the company complies with legal and social environmental regulation and requirements. Furthermore, the firm has to implement programs with environmental objectives and targets and has to assign responsibilities to people to achieve these objectives, targets and time frames.

IMPLEMENTATION AND OPERATION

The firm's management has to ensure that the firm's people can achieve environmental objectives, targets and time frames by allocating resources, such as time, skills, organizational infrastructure, technology and money, to the people who are responsible for environmental care. The firm must ensure that these people have the necessary education, training and experience. The firm must also communicate with stakeholders within the firm and to the stakeholders outside the firm about the functioning of the environmental activities. The firm must keep and maintain records of the environmental management system's policy, procedures and documents. All documents of the system must be up to date, and the documented system must correspond to the actual system in practice. The documented and actual system must be consistent with the firm's environmental policy. The firm must describe how it will deal with cases of environmental emergency.

CHECKING

The firm must use procedures to monitor, measure and ensure that its environmental management procedures correspond to its environmental objectives and targets. It has to plan periodic evaluations of procedures and ensure that these procedures are coherent and consistent and compliant with legal and social requirements. It must keep records of these evaluations. The firm also must have procedures to trace nonconformities and to investigate the causes of these nonconformities. It has to define the need for corrective actions, must record these actions and has to review the effectiveness of the actions. The firm must ensure that all documentation related to environmental policy and procedures is available and accessible. It must plan periodic internal reviews of its environmental policy and procedures to check whether they comply with the requirements of the ISO 14001 standard.

MANAGEMENT REVIEW

The firm's top management has to periodically review the organization's environmental management system to assess and ensure that it is suitable, adequate and effective. Top management has to report opportunities to improve the system and must record the results of the periodic management review. The reports must include the firm's compliance with legal and social requirements, communication with stakeholders, environmental performance, the degree to which environmental objectives and targets are being met, the defined corrective and preventive actions to maintain and improve the environmental management system and recommendations for improvement.

Appendix 3
ISO 14004 Environmental Management Systems—General Guidelines on Principles, Systems and Support Techniques

The ISO 14004 standard (ISO, 2004b) provides a detailed explanation to firms of the possibilities for implementing an environmental management system in the firm that meets the ISO 14001 standard. It consists of guide-lines and practical checklists with examples that enable firms to build their own environmental management system.

ISO 14004 gives principles, systems and support techniques for the ele-ments of an environmental management system that complies with the ISO 14001 norm. These elements are general requirements, environmental policy, planning, implementation and operation, checking and management review.

GENERAL REQUIREMENTS

The environmental management system of the firm has to meet the gen-eral requirements of the ISO 14001 norm by using the plan-do-check-act (PDCA) cycle. In the plan stage, the firm makes plans. In the do stage, the firm does what is planned. In the check stage, the firm assesses and evaluates the results. In the act stage, the firm undertakes corrective and preventive action to improve its operations and results. When the act stage ends, a new plan stage and PDCA cycle start. In essence, the PDCA approach in ISO 14004 is an ongoing, cyclic process of building, maintaining and improving an environmental management system.

ENVIRONMENTAL POLICY

A firm's environmental policy has to describe:

- "its mission, vision, core values and beliefs;
- coordination with other organizational policies (e.g. quality, occupa-tional health and safety);

- the requirements of, and communication with interested parties;
- guiding principles;
- specific local or regional conditions;
- its commitments to prevention of pollution and continual improvement;
- its commitment to comply with legal requirements and other requirements to which the organization subscribes" (p. 9).

PLANNING (PLAN STAGE)

The environmental objectives and targets that need to be defined in the plan stage are, for example, the firm's:

- "emissions to air;
- releases to water;
- releases to land;
- use of raw materials and natural resources (e.g. land use, water use);
- local/community environmental issues;
- use of energy;
- energy emitted (heat, radiation, vibration);
- waste and by-products;
- physical attributes (e.g. size, shape, color, appearance)" (p. 12).

These objectives and targets need to be related to processes of the firm, such as:

- "design and development;
- manufacturing;
- packaging and transportation;
- processes of contractors and suppliers;
- waste management;
- extraction and distribution of raw materials and natural resources;
- distribution, use and end of life;
- wildlife and biodiversity" (p. 12).

To determine the significance of the environmental effects and plan actions, the firm has to consider environmental criteria, including:

- "scale;
- severity and duration of the impact;
- applicable legal requirements;
- the concerns of internal and external interested parties" (p. 13).

Information sources that can be used to determine a firm's environmental aspects and environmental effects are:

- "general information documents, such as brochures, catalogues and annual reports;

- operations manuals, process flowcharts, or quality and product plans;
- reports from previous audits, assessments or reviews, such as initial environmental reviews or life cycle assessments;
- information from other management systems, such as quality or occupational health and safety;
- technical data reports, published analyses or studies, or lists of toxic substances;
- applicable legal requirements and other requirements to which the organization subscribes;
- codes of practice, national and international policies, guidelines and programs;
- purchasing data;
- product specifications, product development data, Material/Chemical Safety Data Sheets (M/CSDS), or energy and material balance data;
- waste inventories;
- monitoring data;
- environmental permit or license applications;
- views of, requests from, or agreements with interested parties;
- reports on emergency situations and accidents" (p. 14).

Legal requirements a firm can include in its plans include:

- "legislation, including statutes and regulations;
- decrees and directives;
- permits, licenses or other forms of authorization;
- orders issued by regulatory agencies;
- judgments of courts or administrative tribunals;
- customary or indigenous law;
- treaties, conventions and protocols" (p. 15).

In addition to legal requirements, an organization can also subscribe to voluntary, social requirements, such as:

- "agreements with public authorities;
- agreements with customers;
- non-regulatory guidelines;
- voluntary principles or codes of practice;
- voluntary environmental labeling or product stewardship commitments;
- requirements of trade associations;
- agreements with community groups or non-governmental organizations;
- public commitments of the organization or its parent organization;
- corporate/company requirements" (p. 15).

The inputs an organization should use while setting objectives and targets are:

- "principles and commitments in its environmental policy;
- its significant environmental aspects;

- applicable legal requirements and other requirements to which the organization subscribes;
- effects of achieving objectives on other activities and processes;
- views of interested parties;
- technological options and feasibility;
- financial, operational, and organizational considerations, including information from suppliers and contractors;
- possible effects on the public image of the organization;
- findings from environmental reviews" (p. 17).

Progress toward environmental objectives can be measured with environmental performance indicators such as:

- "quantity of raw material or energy used;
- quantity of emissions such as CO_2;
- waste produced per quantity of finished product;
- efficiency of material and energy used;
- number of environmental incidents;
- percentage waste recycled;
- percentage recycled material used in packaging;
- number of service vehicle kilometers per unit of production;
- quantities of specific pollutants emitted, e.g., NO_x, SO_2, CO, VOCs, Pb, CFCs;
- investment in environmental protection;
- number of prosecutions;
- land area set aside for wildlife habitat" (p. 19).

IMPLEMENTATION AND OPERATION (DO STAGE)

To ensure that the firm's environmental management systems function appropriately, the firm has to assign responsibilities to its people. A possible responsibility structure is:

- "President, chief executive officer (CEO), board of directors: establish overall direction;
- President, CEO, and others as appropriate: develop environmental policy;
- Top management: review the operation of the environmental management system;
- Relevant managers: develop environmental objectives, targets and programs;
- Chief environmental manager: monitor overall environmental management system performance;
- All managers: assure compliance with applicable legal requirements and other requirements to which the organization subscribes; promote continual improvement;

- Sales and marketing staff: identify customers' expectations;
- Purchasers, buyers: identify requirements for suppliers;
- Finance/accounting managers: develop and maintain accounting procedures;
- All persons working for or on behalf of the organization: conform to environmental management system requirements" (p. 21).

The environmental management system has to control, evaluate and improve the environmental aspects of the firm's operations, such as:

- "acquisition, construction or modification of property and facilities;
- contracting;
- customer service;
- handling and storage of raw materials;
- marketing and advertising;
- production and maintenance processes;
- purchasing;
- research, design, and development engineering;
- storage of products;
- transportation;
- utility processes (e.g. energy and water supply, recycling, waste and wastewater management)" (p. 27).

The procedures, measures and activities with regard to these operations have to be documented, for example in:

- "statements of policy, objectives and targets;
- descriptions of the scope of the environmental management system;
- descriptions of programs and responsibilities;
- information on significant environmental aspects;
- procedures;
- process information;
- organizational charts;
- internal and external standards;
- site emergency plans;
- records" (p. 25).

CHECKING (CHECK STAGE)

An organization has to check the degree to which it is complying with the guidelines and rules it adopted in its environmental management system. Methods that can be used to assess compliance are:

- "audits;
- document and/or records review;

- facility inspections;
- interviews;
- project or work reviews;
- routine sample analysis or test results, and/or verification sampling/testing;
- facility tour and/or direct observation" (p. 29).

MANAGEMENT REVIEW (ACT STAGE)

Continual improvement is a key element of an environmental management system, and periodic management reviews have to result in improvement activities, including:

- "establishing a process for evaluating new materials to promote the use of less harmful materials;
- improving an organization's process for identifying applicable legal requirements so that new compliance requirements are identified in a more timely fashion;
- improving employee training on materials and handling to reduce an organization's generation of waste;
- introducing waste water treatment processes to allow water reuse;
- implementing changes in default settings on reproduction equipment to print two-sided copies at a printing office;
- redesigning delivery routes to reduce fossil fuel consumption by transportation companies;
- setting objectives and targets to implement fuel substitution in boiler operations and reduce particulate emissions" (p. 33).

Appendix 4
ISO 14020 Environmental Labels and Declarations—General Principles

The ISO 14020 norm provides general principles for companies' environmental labels and declarations (ISO, 2000). The norm aims to contribute to the demand for environmentally conscious products and services. The norm's nine general principles require firms to communicate about the environmental aspects of their eco-labeled products in a transparent, verifiable and accurate way. According to ISO 14020:

1. Environmental labels and declarations must be accurate, verifiable, relevant and not misleading.

2. Environmental labels and declarations must not create unnecessary obstacles to international trade.
3. Environmental labels and declarations must be based on scientific methodology.
4. Environmental labels and declarations must be based on a procedure, methodology and criteria that are available and provided upon request.
5. Environmental labels and declarations must take into consideration all relevant aspects of the life cycle of the product.
6. Environmental labels and declarations must not impede ongoing eco-innovation of the product.
7. Environmental labels and declarations must be accompanied by the necessary, and only the necessary, administrative requirements, which enables all organizations, regardless of size, to introduce a label or declaration.
8. Environmental labels and declarations must be developed in open, participatory consultation with interested stakeholders.
9. Environmental labels and declarations must be based on information that is made available to (potential) purchasers of the product.

Appendix 5
ISO 14040 Environmental Management—Life Cycle Assessment—Principles and Frameworks

The ISO 14040 norm describes the principles of and framework for life cycle assessment (LCA) of products (ISO, 2006a). LCA is a scientific methodology that enables organizations to assess and evaluate the environmental impact of products. It is a methodology to specify the environmental aspects of products and to quantify the environmental impact of a product. According to ISO 14040, the eight basic principles of LCA methodology are:

1. Life-cycle perspective: "LCA considers the entire life cycle of a product, from raw material extraction and acquisition, through energy and material production and manufacturing, to use and end of life treatment and final disposal" (pp. 6–7). This means that an LCA aims to consider all operations related to a product.
2. Environmental focus: "LCA addresses the environmental aspects and impacts" (p. 7). This means that only environmental aspects are taken into account.
3. Relative approach and functional unit: "LCA is a relative approach, which is structured around a functional unit" (p. 7). This implies that before an LCA starts, the subject of the LCA must be defined and demarcated.

4. Iterative approach: "The individual phases of an LCA use results of the other phases" (p. 7). This means that calculations build upon calculations and figures that are already available and that apply to the functional unit.
5. Transparency: "Transparency is an important guiding principle in executing LCAs" (p. 7). This means that because of the complexity of an LCA, all information and procedures have to be available and transparent. This enables an accurate interpretation of the results.
6. Comprehensiveness: "LCA considers all attributes or aspects of natural environment, human health and resources" (p. 7). This implies that an LCA provides an overview of all environmental effects and a weighting of their relative impact.
7. Priority of scientific approach: "Decisions within an LCA are preferably based on natural science. If this is not possible, other scientific approaches (e.g. from social and economic sciences) may be used or international conventions may be referred to. If neither a scientific basis exists nor a justification based on other scientific approaches or international conventions is possible, then, as appropriate, decisions may be based on value choices" (p. 7). This implies that it is preferable but not necessary that an LCA is based on specified, scientific methods.
8. General: "These principles are fundamental and should be used as guidance for decisions relating to both the planning and the conducting of an LCA" (p. 6).

The following list of some of the key features of LCA methodology implies that LCA is preferably based on science, scientific method and an objective approach and thus aims at the highest degree of objectivity, certainty and accuracy. Despite this, it also implies that the LCA is an instrument or approach that carries a certain degree of subjectivity, uncertainty and inaccuracy:

• "the depth of detail and time frame of an LCA may vary to a large extent, depending on the goal and scope definition;
• provisions are made, depending on the intended application of the LCA, to respect confidentiality and proprietary matters;
• LCA methodology is open to the inclusion of new scientific findings and improvements in the state-of-the-art of the technique;
• specific requirements are applied to LCA that are intended to be used in comparative assertions intended to be disclosed to the public;
• there is no single method for conducting LCA. Organizations have the flexibility to implement LCA as established in the ISO 14040 standard, in accordance with the intended application and the requirements of the organization;

- LCA addresses potential environmental impacts; LCA does not predict absolute or precise environmental impacts due to: the relative expression of potential environmental impacts to a reference unit; the integration of environmental data over space and time; the inherent uncertainty in modeling of environmental impacts; and the fact that some possible environmental impacts are clearly future impacts;
- there is no scientific basis for reducing LCA results to a single overall score or number, since weighting requires value choices;
- life cycle interpretation uses a systematic procedure to identify, qualify, check, evaluate and present the conclusions based on the findings of an LCA, in order to meet the requirements of the application as described in the goal and scope of the study" (pp. 8–9).

Appendix 6
ISO/TR 14062 Environmental Management— Integrating Environmental Aspects into Product Design and Development

The ISO/TR (Technical Report) 14062 provides guidelines for integrating environmental aspects into product design and development (ISO, 2002). The standard looks at the environmental aspects of new products from an input-output perspective. It states that the environmental impacts of a product's input stage, that is, the use of materials and energy, and output stage, including emissions and other releases, have to be taken into account and have to be reduced.

INPUTS

For inputs, the technical report distinguishes two categories: material inputs and energy inputs.

Material inputs are divided into nonrenewable and renewable resources. Environmental aspects of material inputs in the design process are the exposure of humans and ecological systems to contaminants, emissions to air, water and soil, and the generation of waste materials. The basic idea is that product design and development aims at the use of renewable resources, a reduction in the use of nonrenewable resources and reduced emissions and other releases to the environment.

Energy inputs include fossil and biomass fuels, nuclear power, hydropower and geothermal, solar and wind energy. Each type of energy has identifiable environmental aspects, such as CO_2 emissions and depletion of fossil fuel supplies. The basic concept of eco-aware design and development of products is that these products can be produced with reduced or no emissions and with renewable energy sources.

OUTPUTS

The outputs of the product development and design process are generated during the product's life cycle. Examples of outputs are air emissions, effluent discharges, solid and liquid waste materials and other releases:

- Air emissions: releases of gases, vapors and other matters into the air. "These releases may adversely affect ecosystems, people, materials or contribute to other adverse environmental impacts such as acidification, ozone depletion, and climate change" (p. 13).
- Effluent discharges: "discharges of substances to waterways, either surface or groundwater. Like air emissions, these discharges could adversely affect the environment" (p. 13).
- Waste materials: "solid or liquid waste products can become inputs to other processes or can be treated, recycled, used as energy sources, incinerated or landfilled" (p. 13).
- Other releases: "noise, radiation, and electromagnetic fields, etc." (p. 13).

The basic concept of eco-friendly product design and development is that harmful emissions, discharges and waste of products with respect to use and disposal are taken into account. This information is used to design and develop products with limited or no detrimental impacts on the environment.

Appendix 7
ISO 26000 Guidance on Social Responsibility

The final draft of the ISO 26000 norm provides guidance on corporate social responsibility (ISO, 2010). It defines and describes guidelines for seven core subjects of corporate sustainability: organizational governance, human rights, labor practices, the environment, fair operating practices, consumer issues, and community involvement and development.

1   ORGANIZATIONAL GOVERNANCE

"Organizational governance is the most crucial factor in enabling an organization to take responsibility for the impacts of its decisions and activities and to integrate social responsibility throughout the organization and its relationships" (p. 21).

2 HUMAN RIGHTS

"Recognition and respect for human rights are widely regarded as essential to the rule of law and to concepts of social justice and fairness and as the basic underpinning of the most essential institutions of society such as the judicial system" (p. 24). The human-rights subject consists of eight issues.

2.1 Due Diligence

"To respect human rights, organizations have a responsibility to exercise due diligence to identify, prevent and address actual or potential human rights impacts resulting from their activities or the activities of those with which they have relationships" (p. 25).

2.2 Human-Rights Risk Situations

"There are certain circumstances and environments where organizations are more likely to face challenges and dilemmas relating to human rights and in which the risk of human rights abuse may be exacerbated" (p. 25). "Organizations should take particular care when dealing with [these] situations" (p. 26).

2.3 Avoidance of Complicity

Organizations should avoid complicity in unethical or improper acts. "An organization may be considered complicit when it assists in the commission of wrongful acts of others that are inconsistent with, or disrespectful of, international norms of behavior that the organization, through exercising due diligence, knew or should have known would lead to substantial negative impacts on society, the economy or the environment" (p. 26).

2.4 Resolution of Grievances

"To discharge its responsibility to respect human rights, an organization should establish a mechanism for those who believe their human rights have been abused to bring this to the attention of the organization and seek redress" (p. 27).

2.5 Discrimination and Vulnerable Groups

"The full and effective participation and inclusion in society of all groups, including those who are vulnerable, provides and increases opportunities for all organizations as well as the people concerned. An organization has much to gain from taking an active approach to ensuring equal opportunity and respect for all individuals" (p. 28).

2.6 Civil and Political Rights

"An organization should respect all individual civil and political rights" (p. 30), including "life of individuals, freedom of opinion, expression, peaceful assembly, information exchange, the right to own property, and access to due process and the right to a fair hearing before any internal disciplinary measure is taken" (p. 30).

2.7 Economic, Social and Cultural Rights

"Every person, as a member of society, has economic, social and cultural rights necessary for his or her dignity and personal development. . . . To respect these rights, an organization has a responsibility to exercise due diligence to ensure that it does not engage in activities that infringe, obstruct or impede the enjoyment of such rights" (p. 30).

2.8 Fundamental Principles and Rights at Work

"An organization should independently ensure that it addresses the following matters: freedom of association and collective bargaining, . . . forced labor, . . . equal opportunities . . . and non-discrimination, child labor" (pp. 31–32).

3 LABOR PRACTICES

"The creation of jobs, as well as wages and other compensation paid for work performed, are among an organization's most important economic and social contributions" (p. 34). The labor practices subject consists of five issues.

3.1 Employment and Employment Relationships

"The employment relationship confers rights and imposes obligations on both employers and employees in the interest of both the organization and society" (p. 35).

3.2 Conditions of Work and Social Protection

"Fair and appropriate consideration should be given to the quality of conditions of work. . . . Conditions of work include wages and other forms of compensation, working time, rest periods, holidays, disciplinary and dismissal practices, maternity protection and welfare matters such as safe drinking water, sanitation, canteens and access to medical services" (p. 36).

3.3   Social Dialogue

"Social dialogue includes all types of negotiation, consultation or exchange of information between or among representatives of governments, employers and workers, on matters of common interest relating to economic and social concerns. It could take place between employer and worker representatives, on matters affecting their interests" (p. 37).

3.4   Health and Safety at Work

"Health and safety at work concerns the promotion and maintenance of the highest degree of physical, mental and social well-being of workers and prevention of harm to health caused by working conditions. It also relates to the protection of workers from risks to health and the adaptation of the occupational environment to the physiological and psychological needs of workers" (p. 38).

3.5   Human Development and Training in the Workplace

"Human development includes the process of enlarging people's choices by expanding human capabilities and functioning, thus enabling women and men to lead long and healthy lives, to be knowledgeable and to have a decent standard of living" (p. 40).

4   THE ENVIRONMENT

"Environmental responsibility is a precondition for the survival and prosperity of human beings. It is therefore an important aspect of social responsibility. . . . Society is facing many environmental challenges, including the depletion of natural resources, pollution, climate change, destruction of habitats, loss of species, the collapse of whole ecosystems and the degradation of urban and rural human settlements. As the world population grows and consumption increases, these changes are increasing threats to human security and the health and well being of society. There is a need to identify options to reduce and eliminate unsustainable patterns of production and consumption and to ensure that the resource consumption per person becomes sustainable. Environmental matters at the local, regional and global level are interconnected. Addressing them requires a comprehensive, systematic and collective approach" (p. 41). The environment subject consists of four issues.

4.1 Prevention of Pollution

"An organization can improve its environmental performance by preventing pollution, including: emissions to air, . . . discharges to water, . . . waste management, . . . use and disposal of toxic and hazardous chemicals, . . . other identifiable forms of pollution" (pp. 42–43).

4.2 Sustainable Resource Use

"An organization can progress towards sustainable resource use by using electricity, fuels, raw and processed materials, land and water more responsibly, and by combining or replacing non-renewable resources with sustainable, renewable resources" (p. 44).

4.3 Climate Change Mitigation and Adaptation

"It is recognized that emissions of greenhouse gases (GHG) from human activities, such as carbon dioxide (CO_2), methane (CH_4) and nitrous oxide (N_2O), are very likely one of the causes of global climate change, which is having significant impacts on the natural and human environment. . . . Every organization is responsible for some GHG emissions (either directly or indirectly) and will be affected in some way by climate change" (p. 45).

4.4 Protection of the Environment, Biodiversity and Restoration of Natural Habitats

"An organization can become more socially responsible by acting to protect the environment and restore natural habitats and the various functions and services that ecosystems provide (such as food and water, climate regulation, soil formation and recreational opportunities). . . . Key aspects of this issue include: valuing and protecting biodiversity, . . . valuing, protecting and restoring ecosystem services, . . . using land and natural resource sustainably, . . . advancing environmentally sound urban and rural development" (pp. 46–47).

5   FAIR OPERATING PRACTICES

"Fair operating practices concern the way an organization uses its relationships with other organizations to promote positive outcomes. Positive outcomes can be achieved by providing leadership and promoting the adoption of social responsibility more broadly throughout the organization's sphere of influence" (p. 48). The fair operating practices subject consists of five issues.

5.1 Anticorruption Practices

Firms must be anticorruption. "Corruption is the abuse of entrusted power for private gain. Corruption can take many forms. Examples of corruption include bribery (soliciting, offering or accepting a bribe in money or in kind) involving public officials or people in the private sector, conflict of interest, fraud, money laundering, embezzlement, concealment and obstruction of justice, and trading in influence" (p. 48).

5.2 Responsible Political Involvement

"Organizations can support public political processes and encourage the development of public policy that benefits society at large. Organizations should prohibit use of undue influence and avoid behavior, such as manipulation, intimidation and coercion that can undermine the public political process" (p. 49).

5.3 Fair Competition

"Fair and widespread competition stimulates innovation and efficiency, reduces the costs of products and services, ensures all organizations have equal opportunities, encourages the development of new or improved products or processes and, in the long run, enhances economic growth and living standards. Anti-competitive behavior risks harming the reputation of an organization with its stakeholders and may create legal problems. When organizations refuse to engage in anti-competitive behavior they help to build a climate in which such behavior is not tolerated, and this benefits everyone" (p. 49).

5.4 Promotion of Social Responsibility in the Value Chain

"An organization should consider the potential impacts or unintended consequences of its procurement and purchasing decisions on other organizations, and take due care to avoid or minimize any negative impacts" (p. 50).

5.5 Respect for Property Rights

Firms must respect human property rights. "The right to own property is a human right recognized in the Universal Declaration of Human Rights. Property rights cover both physical property and intellectual property and include interest in land and other physical assets, copyrights, patents, geographical indicator rights, funds, moral rights and other rights" (p. 51).

6 CONSUMER ISSUES

"Consumer issues regarding social responsibility are related to, among other matters, fair marketing practices, protection of health and safety, sustainable consumption, dispute resolution and redress, data and privacy protection, access to essential products and services, addressing the needs of vulnerable and disadvantaged consumers, and education" (p. 52). The consumer subject consists of seven issues.

6.1 Fair Marketing, Factual and Unbiased Information and Fair Contractual Practices

"Fair marketing, factual and unbiased information and fair contractual practices provide information about products and services in a manner that can be understood by consumers" (p. 53).

6.2 Protection of Consumers' Health and Safety

"Protection of consumers' health and safety involves the provision of products and services that are safe and that do not carry unacceptable risk of harm when used or consumed" (p. 55).

6.3 Sustainable Consumption

Firms should contribute to sustainable consumption. "Sustainable consumption is consumption of products and resources at rates consistent with sustainable development" (p. 55).

6.4 Consumer Service, Support, and Complaint and Dispute Resolution

"Consumer service, support, and complaint and dispute resolution are the mechanisms an organization uses to address the needs of consumers after products and services are bought or provided. Such mechanisms include proper installation, warranties and guarantees, technical support regarding use, as well as provisions for return, repair and maintenance" (p. 57).

6.5 Consumer Data Protection and Privacy

"Consumer data protection and privacy are intended to safeguard consumers' rights of privacy by limiting the types of information gathered and the ways in which such information is obtained, used and secured" (p. 58).

6.6 Access to Essential Services

"Although the state is responsible for ensuring that the right to satisfaction of basic needs is respected, there are many locations or conditions in which the state does not ensure that this right is protected. Even where satisfaction of some basic needs, such as health care, is protected, the right to essential utility services, such as electricity, gas, water, wastewater services, drainage, sewage and communication may not be fully achieved. An organization can contribute to the fulfillment of this right" (p. 59).

6.7 Education and Awareness

Firms must contribute to education and awareness. "Education and awareness initiatives enable consumers to be well informed, conscious of their rights and responsibilities, more likely to assume an active role and to be able to make knowledgeable purchasing decisions and consume responsibly" (p. 59).

7 COMMUNITY INVOLVEMENT AND DEVELOPMENT

"It is widely accepted today that organizations have a relationship with the communities in which they operate. This relationship should be based on community involvement so as to contribute to community development" (p. 60). The community involvement and development subject consists of seven issues.

7.1 Community Involvement

"Community involvement is an organization's proactive outreach to the community. It is aimed at preventing and solving problems, fostering partnerships with local organizations and stakeholders and aspiring to be a good organizational citizen of the community" (p. 63).

7.2 Education and Culture

Firms contribute to education and culture. "Preservation and promotion of culture and promotion of education compatible with respect for human rights have positive impacts on social cohesion and development" (p. 64).

7.3 Employment Creation and Skills Development

"Employment is an internationally recognized objective related to economic and social development. By creating employment, all organizations, large and small, can make a contribution to reducing poverty and promoting economic and social development" (p. 65).

7.4   Technology Development and Access

"To help advance economic and social development, communities and their members need, among other things, full and safe access to modern technology. Organizations can contribute to the development of the communities in which they operate by applying specialized knowledge, skills and technology in such a way as to promote human resource development and technology diffusion" (p. 65).

7.5   Wealth and Income Creation

"Competitive and diverse enterprises and co-operatives are crucial in creating wealth in any community. Organizations can help to create an environment in which entrepreneurship can thrive, bringing lasting benefits to communities" (p. 66).

7.6   Health

"Health is an essential element of life in society and is a recognized human right. Threats to public health can have severe impacts on communities and can hamper their development. Thus, all organizations, both large and small, should respect the right to health and should contribute, within their means and as appropriate, to the promotion of health, to the prevention of health threats and diseases and to the mitigation of any damage to the community" (p. 67).

7.7   Social Investment

"Social investment takes place when organizations invest their resources in initiatives and programs aimed at improving social aspects of community life. Types of social investments may include projects related to education, training, culture, health care, income generation, infrastructure development, improving access to information or any other activity likely to promote economic or social development" (p. 68).

Bibliography

Abernethy, M.A., Bouwens, J., Van Lent, L. (2010) Leadership and control system design. *Management Accounting Research*, 21(1): 2–16.

Acha, V., Gann, D., Salter, A. (2005) Episodic innovation: R&D strategies for project-based environments. *Industry and Innovation*, 12(2): 255–282.

Adarves-Yorno, I., Postmes, T., Haslam, S.A. (2007) Creative innovation or crazy irrelevance? The contribution of group norms and social identity to creative behavior. *Journal of Experimental Social Psychology*, 43(3): 410–416.

Aggeri, F., Segrestin, B. (2007) Innovation and project development: An impossible equation? Lessons from an innovative automobile project development. *R&D Management*, 37(1): 37–48.

Ählström, J., Sjöström, E. (2005) CSOs and business partnerships: Strategies for interaction. *Business Strategy and the Environment*, 14(4): 230–240.

Al-Saleh, Y.M., Taleb, H.M. (2010) The integration of sustainability within value management practices: A study of experienced value managers in the GCC countries. *Project Management Journal*, 41(2): 50–59.

Andersson, H., Berggren, C. (2007) Individual inventors in the R&D factory. *Creativity and Innovation Management*, 16(4): 437–446.

Avery, G.C., Bergsteiner, H. (2011a) How BMW successfully practices sustainable leadership principles. *Strategy & Leadership*, 39(6): 11–18.

Avery, G.C., Bergsteiner, H. (2011b) Sustainable leadership practices for enhancing business resilience and performance. *Strategy & Leadership*, 39(3): 5–15.

Baraldi, E., Strömsten, T. (2009) Controlling and combining resources in networks—From Uppsala to Stanford, and back again: The case of a biotech innovation. *Industrial Marketing Management*, 38(5): 541–552.

Barlow, J. (2000) Innovation and learning in complex offshore construction projects. *Research Policy*, 29(7–8): 973–989.

Barney, J. (1991) Firm resources and sustained competitive advantage. *Journal of Management*, 17(1): 99–120.

Bartholomew, S. (1997) National systems of biotechnology innovation: Complex interdependence in the global system. *Journal of International Business Studies*, 28(2): 241–266.

Berkhout, A.J., Hartmann, D., Trott, P. (2010) Connecting technological capabilities with market needs using a cyclic innovation model. *R&D Management*, 40(5): 474–490.

Beveridge, R., Guy, S. (2005) The rise of the eco-preneur and the messy world of environmental innovation. *Local Environment*, 10(6): 665–676.

Beverland, M.B. (2005) Managing the design innovation-brand marketing interface: Resolving the tension between artistic creation and commercial imperatives. *Journal of Product Innovation Management*, 22(2): 193–207.

Bianchi, G. (1996) Galileo used to live here. Tuscany high tech: The networks and its poles. *R&D Management*, 26(3): 199–212.

Bingham, C.B., Eisenhardt, K.M. (2008) Position, leverage and opportunity: A typology of strategic logics linking resources with competitive advantage. *Managerial and Decision Economics*, 19(2): 241–256.

Bissola, R., Imperatori, B (2011) Organizing individual and collective creativity: Flying in the face of creativity clichés. *Creativity and Innovation Management*, 20(2): 77–89.

Björkman, H. (2004) Design dialogue groups as a source of innovation: Factors behind group creativity. *Creativity and Innovation Management*, 13(2): 97–108.

Bjørnåli, E.S., Gulbrandsen, M. (2010) Adverse selection and financing innovation: Is there a need for R&D subsidies? *Journal of Technology Transfer*, 35(1): 16–42.

Blackburn, W.R. (2007) *The Sustainability Handbook*. London: Earthscan, p. 803.

Blindenbach-Driessen, F., Van den Ende, J. (2006) Innovation in project-based firms: The context dependency of success factors. *Research Policy*, 35(4): 545–561.

Boh, W.F. (2007) Mechanisms for sharing knowledge in project-based organizations. *Information and Organization*, 17(1): 27–58.

Bönte, W., Keilbach, M. (2005) Concubinage or marriage? Informal and formal cooperations for innovation. *International Journal of Industrial Organization*, 23(3–4): 279–302.

Bossink, B.A.G. (2002a) A Dutch public–private strategy for innovation in sustainable construction. *Construction Management and Economics*, 20(7): 633–642.

Bossink, B.A.G. (2002b) Innovative quality management practices in the Dutch construction industry. *International Journal of Quality and Reliability Management*, 19(2–3): 170–186.

Bossink, B.A.G. (2002c) The development of co-innovation strategies: Stages and interaction patterns in interfirm innovation. *R&D Management*, 32(4): 311–320.

Bossink, B.A.G. (2004a) Effectiveness of innovation leadership styles: A manager's influence on ecological innovation in construction projects. *Construction Innovation*, 4(4): 211–228.

Bossink, B.A.G. (2004b) Managing drivers of innovation in construction networks. *Journal of Construction Engineering and Management*, 130(3): 337–345.

Bossink, B.A.G. (2007a) Leadership for sustainable innovation. *International Journal of Technology Management and Sustainable Development*, 6(2): 135–149.

Bossink, B.A.G. (2007b) The interorganizational innovation processes of sustainable building: A Dutch case of joint building innovation in sustainability. *Building and Environment*, 42(12): 4086–4092.

Bossink, B.A.G. (2008) Interdependent sustainable innovation processes and systems in Dutch residential building. *Journal of Green Building*, 3(1): 139–155.

Bossink, B.A.G. (2009a) Assessment of a national innovation system of sustainable innovation in residential construction: A case study from the Netherlands. *International Journal of Environmental Technology and Management*, 10(3–4): 371–381.

Bossink, B.A.G. (2009b) Nation-wide development of sustainable production patterns. The case of 16 years of sustainability in Dutch residential house building. *International Journal of Global Environmental Issues*, 9(4): 356–372.

Bossink, B.A.G. (2011a) *Managing Environmentally Sustainable Innovation: Insights from the Construction Industry*. New York: Routledge, p. 192.

Bossink, B.A.G. (2011b) Entrepreneurship for environmentally sustainable design. In: Van Gelderen, M., Masurel, E. (eds.) *Entrepreneurship in Context*. New York: Routledge, pp. 76–86.

Bossink, B.A.G., Brouwers, H.J.H. (1996) Construction waste: Quantification and source evaluation. *Journal of Construction Engineering and Management*, 122(1): 55–60.

Brady, T., Davies, A. (2004) Building project capabilities: From exploratory to exploitative learning. *Organization Studies*, 25(9): 1601–1621.

Brennan, A., Dooley, L. (2005) Networked creativity: A structured management framework for stimulating innovation. *Technovation*, 25(12): 1388–1399.

Brío, J.A., Junquera, B. (2003) A review of the literature on environmental innovation management in SMEs: Implications for public policies. *Technovation*, 23(12): 939–948.

Brockhoff, M.W.J. (2011) *The Role of Leadership in CSR and Its Effect on Organizational Commitment: A Case Study in the Horticulture Sector*. M.Sc. thesis VU University Amsterdam.

Brundtland, G.H., Khalid, S. (1987) *Our Common Future*. Oxford: Oxford University Press, p. 400.

Burgelman, R.A., Christensen, C.M., Wheelwright, S.C. (2004) *Strategic Management of Technology and Innovation*. New York: McGraw-Hill, p. 1208.

Burton, R.M., Obel, B. (1998) *Strategic Organizational Diagnosis and Design*. Norwell Mass.: Kluwer Academic Publishers, p. 445.

Cacciatori, E. (2008) Memory objects in project environments: Storing, retrieving and adapting learning in project-based firms. *Research Policy*, 37(9): 1591–1601.

Calia, R.C., Guerrini, F.M., Moura, G.L. (2007) Innovation networks: From technological development to business model reconfiguration. *Technovation*, 27(8): 426–432.

Carmeli, A., Gelbard, R., Gefen, D. (2010) The importance of innovation leadership in cultivating strategic fit and enhancing firm performance. *Leadership Quarterly*, 21(3): 339–349.

Carson, R. (1962) *Silent Spring*. Boston: Houghton Mifflin, p. 368.

Casey, V. (2009) The designer's dilemma. *Design Management Review*, 20(1): 59–64.

Cetindamar, D. (2003) The diffusion of environmental technologies: The case of the Turkish fertiliser industry. *International Journal of Technology Management*, 26(1): 68–87.

Chesbrough, H. (2010) Business model innovation: Opportunities and barriers. *Long Range Planning*, 43(2–3): 354–363.

Chiesa, V., Manzini, R. (1998) Organizing for technological collaborations: A managerial perspective. *R&D Management*, 28(3): 199–212.

Chiffoleau, Y. (2005) Learning about innovation through networks: The development of environment-friendly viticulture. *Technovation*, 25(10): 1193–1204.

Christensen, J.F., Olesen, M.H., Kjær, J.S. (2005) The industrial dynamics of open innovation-Evidence from the transformation of consumer electronics. *Research Policy*, 34(10): 1533–1549.

Clark, W.W., Paolucci, E. (2001) Commercial development of environmental technologies for the automotive industry: Towards a new model of technological innovation. *International Journal of Technology Management*, 21(5–6): 565–585.

Coakes, E., Smith, P. (2007) Developing communities of innovation by identifying innovation champions. *The Learning Organization*, 14(1): 74–85.

Cohen, W.M., Levinthal, D.A. (1990) Absorptive capacity: A new perspective on learning and innovation. *Administrative Science Quarterly*, 35(1): 128–152.

Crevani, L., Lindgren, M., Packendorff, J. (2010) Leadership, not leaders: On the study of leadership as practices and interactions. *Scandinavian Journal of Management*, 26(1): 77–86.

Dacin, M.T., Dacin, P.A., Tracey, P. (2011) Social entrepreneurship: A critique and future directions. *Organization Science*, 22(5): 1203–1213.

Dammann, S., Elle, M. (2006) Environmental indicators: Establishing a common language for green building. *Building Research & Information*, 34(4): 387–404.

De Bruijn, C.P.T. (2009) *(Successful) Cooperation between Different Actors (Public and Private Sector and NGOs) to Stimulate Innovation for Environmental Sustainability in Dutch Food Industry*. M.Sc. thesis VU University Amsterdam.

De Hoogh, A.H.B., Den Hartog, D.N. (2008) Ethical and despotic leadership, relationships with leader's social responsibility, top management team effectiveness and subordinates' optimism: A multi-method study. *The Leadership Quarterly*, 19(3): 297–311.

Dell'Era, C., Verganti, R. (2009) The impact of international designers on firm innovation capability and consumer interest. *International Journal of Operations and Production Management*, 29(9): 870–893.

De Man, A.P., Duysters, G. (2005) Collaboration and innovation: A review of the effects of mergers, acquisitions and alliances on innovation. *Technovation*, 25(12): 1377–1387.

De Swaaf, K. (2008) *A National Environmental Policy Planning: Development and Implementation in the Dutch FMCG-Food Market*. M.Sc. thesis VU University Amsterdam.

Dewick, P., Miozzo, M. (2004) Networks and innovation: Sustainable technologies in Scottish social housing. *R&D Management*, 34(4): 323–333.

Di Domenico, M.L., Haugh, H. (2007) Strategic partnering: Results from a survey of social ventures in the UK, paper presented at *Conference ISERC-3*, Business School, Copenhagen, June 18–19.

Dixon, S.E.A., Clifford, A. (2007) Ecopreneurship—A new approach to managing the triple bottom line. *Journal of Organizational Change Management*, 20(3): 326–345.

Donnelly, K., Olds, R., Blechinger, F., Reynolds, D., Beckett-Furnell, Z. (2004) ISO 14001—Effective management of sustainable design. *Journal of Sustainable Product Design*, 4(1): 43–54.

Dorenbosch, L., Van Engen, M.L., Verhagen, M. (2005) On-the-job innovation: The impact of job design and human resource management through production ownership. *Creativity and Innovation Management*, 14(2): 129–141.

Dougherty, D. (2008) Bridging social constraint and social action to design organizations for innovation. *Organization Studies*, 29(3): 415–434.

Eisenbeiss, S.A., Van Knippenberg, D., Boerner, S. (2008) Transformational leadership and team innovation: Integrating team climate principles. *Journal of Applied Psychology*, 93(6): 1438–1445.

Esty, D.C., Levy, M., Srebotnjak, T., De Sherbinin, A. (2005) *2005 Environmental Sustainability Index: Benchmarking National Environmental Stewardship*. New Haven: Yale Center for Environmental Law and Policy, p. 403.

Fernando, M., Sim, A.B. (2011) Strategic ambiguity and leaders' responsibility beyond maximizing profits. *European Management Journal*, 29(6): 504–513.

Fisher, M.M., Varga, A. (2002) Technological innovation and interfirm cooperation: An exploratory analysis using survey data from manufacturing firms in the metropolitan region of Vienna. *International Journal of Technology Management*, 24(7–8): 724–742.

Fleming, L., Waguespack, D.M. (2007) Brokerage, boundary spanning, and leadership in open innovation communities. *Organization Science*, 18(2): 165–180.

Fowler, S.J., Hope, C. (2007) Incorporating sustainable business practices into company strategy. *Business Strategy and the Environment*, 16(1): 26–38.

Foxon, T.J., Gross, R., Chase, A., Howes, J., Arnall, A., Anderson, D. (2005) UK innovation systems for new and renewable energy technologies: Drivers, barriers and systems failure. *Energy Policy*, 33(16): 2123–2137.

Gann, D.M., Salter, A.M. (2000) Innovation in project-based, service-enhanced firms: The construction of complex products and systems. *Research Policy*, 29(7–8): 955–972.

Gann, D.M., Wang, Y., Hawkins, R. (1998) Do regulations encourage innovation? The case of energy efficiency in housing. *Building Research & Information*, 26(4): 280–296.

Garvin, M.J., Bosso, D. (2008) Assessing the effectiveness of infrastructure public-private partnership programs and projects. *Public Works Management and Policy*, 13(2): 162–178.

Gemünden, H.G., Salomo, S., Hölzle, K. (2007) Role models for radical innovations in times of open innovation. *Creativity and Innovation Management*, 16(4): 408–421.

George, V.P., Farris, G. (1999) Performance of alliances: Formative stages and changing organizational and environmental influences. *R&D Management*, 29(4): 379–390.

Gladwin, T.N., Kennelly, J.J., Krause, T.S. (1995) Shifting paradigms for sustainable development: Implications for management theory and practice. *Academy of Management Review*, 20(4): 874–907.

Gluch, P., Stenberg, A.C. (2006) How do trade media influence green building practice? *Building Research & Information*, 34(2): 104–117.

Gore, A. (2006) *An Inconvenient Truth*. New York: Rodale, p. 328.

Goverse, T., Hekkert, M.P., Groenewegen, P., Worrell, E., Smits, R.E.H.M. (2001). Wood innovation in the residential construction sector: Opportunities and constraints. *Resources, Conservation and Recycling*, 34(1): 53–74.

Green, D.D., McCann, J. (2011) Benchmarking a leadership model for the green economy. *Benchmarking: An International Journal*, 18(3): 445–465.

Håkanson, L. (1993) Managing cooperative research and development: Partner selection and contract design. *R&D Management*, 23(4): 273–286.

Halbesleben, J.R.B., Novicevic, M.M., Harvey, M.G., Buckley, M.R. (2003) Awareness of temporal complexity in leadership of creativity and innovation: A competency-based model. *Leadership Quarterly*, 14(4): 433–454.

Harborne, P., Hendry, C. (2009) Pathways to commercial wind power in the US, Europe and Japan: The role of demonstration projects and field trials in the innovation process. *Energy Policy*, 37(9): 3580–3595.

Hart, S.L. (1995) A natural-resource-based view of the firm. *Academy of Management Review*, 20(4): 986–1014.

Hauschildt, J., Kirchmann, E. (2001) Teamwork for innovation: The troika of promoters. *R&D Management*, 31(1): 41–49.

Hawken, P. (1993) *The Ecology of Commerce: A Declaration of Sustainability*. New York: Harper Business, p. 250.

Hendry, C., Harborne, P., Brown, J. (2010) So what do innovating companies really get from publicly funded demonstration projects and trials? Innovation lessons from solar photovoltaics and wind. *Energy Policy*, 38(8): 4507–4519.

Howell, J.M., Boies, K. (2004) Champions of technological innovation: The influence of contextual knowledge, role orientation, idea generation, and idea promotion on champion emergence. *Leadership Quarterly*, 15(1): 123–144.

Hülsheger, U.R., Anderson, N., Salgado, J.F. (2009) Team-level predictors of innovation at work: A comprehensive meta-analysis spanning three decades of research. *Journal of Applied Psychology*, 94(5): 1128–1144.

Indriani, M.T.D. (2009) *Strategic Cooperation for Sustainable Innovations: New Market Creation*. M.Sc. thesis VU University Amsterdam.

ISO (2000) International Standard 14020: *Environmental Labels and Declarations—General Principles*, p. 5.

ISO (2002) *Technical Report 14062: Environmental Management—Integrating Environmental Aspects into Product Design and Development*, p. 25.

ISO (2004a) *International Standard 14001: Environmental Management Systems—Requirements with Guidance for Use*, p. 23.

ISO (2004b) *International Standard 14004: Environmental Management Systems—General Guidelines on Principles, Systems and Support Techniques*, p. 39.

ISO (2006a) *International Standard 14040: Environmental Management—Life Cycle Assessment—Principles and Framework*, p. 20.

ISO (2010) *International Standard 26000: Guidance on Social Responsibility*, p. 106.

Jung, D., Wu, A., Chow, C.W. (2008) Towards understanding the direct and indirect effects of CEOs' transformational leadership on firm innovation. *Leadership Quarterly*, 19(5): 582–594.

Kangari, R., Miyatake, Y. (1997) Developing and managing innovative construction technologies in Japan. *Journal of Construction Engineering and Management*, 123(1): 72–78.

Kassinis, G., Vafeas, N. (2006) Stakeholder pressures and environmental performance. *Academy of Management Journal*, 49(1): 145–159.

Keegan, A., Turner, J.R. (2002) The management of innovation in project-based firms. *Long Range Planning*, 35(4): 367–388.

Kelley, D., Lee, H. (2010) Managing innovation champions: The impact of project characteristics on the direct manager role. *Journal of Product Innovation Management*, 27(7): 1007–1020.

Kenny, J. (2003) Effective project management for strategic innovation and change in an organizational context. *Project Management Journal*, 34(1): 43–53.

Keoleian, G.A., Kar, K. (2003) Elucidating complex design and management tradeoffs through life cycle design: Air intake manifold demonstration project. *Journal of Cleaner Production*, 11(1): 61–77.

Killen, C.P., Hunt, R.A., Kleinschmidt, E.J. (2008) Project portfolio management for product innovation. *International Journal of Quality and Reliability Management*, 25(1): 24–38.

King, A. (1995) Avoiding ecological surprise: Lessons from long-standing communities. *Academy of Management Review*, 20(4): 961–985.

Kivimaa, P., Mickwitz, P. (2006) The challenge of greening technologies: Environmental policy integration in Finnish technology policies. *Research Policy*, 35(5): 729–744.

Klawer, C.G. (2008) *Sustainable Development: No Time to Waste, the Future Is Now*. M.Sc. thesis VU University Amsterdam.

Klein Woolthuis, R.J. (2009) Sustainable entrepreneurship in the Dutch construction industry. *Sustainability*, 2(2): 505–523.

Kratzer, J., Leenders, R.Th.A.J., Van Engelen, J.M.L. (2006) Team polarity and creative performance in innovation teams. *Creativity and Innovation Management*, 15(1): 96–104.

Kreiner, K., Schulz, M. (1993) Informal collaboration in R&D: The formation of networks across organizations. *Organization Studies*, 14(2): 189–209.

Krozer, J., Mass, K., Kothuis, B. (2003) Demonstration of environmentally sound and cost-effective shipping. *Journal of Cleaner Production*, 11(7): 767–777.

Kunz, V.D., Warren, L. (2011) From innovation to market entry: A strategic management model for new technologies. *Technology Analysis and Strategic Management*, 23(4): 345–367.

Labuschagne, C., Brent, A.C. (2005) Sustainable project life cycle management: The need to integrate life cycles in the manufacturing sector. *International Journal of Project Management*, 23(10): 159–168.

Labuschagne, C., Brent, A.C. (2008) An industry perspective of the completeness and relevance of a social assessment framework for project and technology management in the manufacturing sector. *Journal of Cleaner Production*, 16(3): 253–262.

Lejano, R.P., Davos, C.A. (1999) Cooperative solutions for sustainable resource management. *Environmental Management*, 24(2): 167–175.

Lovelock, J. (1980) *Gaia: A New Look at Life on Earth*. Oxford: Oxford University Press, p. 176.

Lundvall, B.-Å., Johnson, B., Andersen, E.S., Dalum, B. (2002) National systems of production, innovation and competence building. *Research Policy*, 31(2): 213–231.

MacDonald, S., Piekkari, R. (2005) Out of control: Personal networks in European collaboration. *R&D Management*, 35(4): 441–453.

Mahawat Khan, A. (2010) *Contributions to the Function Approach of System Innovation: A Functions Approach Exploring the Key Success Factors That Enable a Transition towards Sustainability.* M.Sc. thesis VU University Amsterdam.

Manfredi, S., Pant, R., Pennington, D.W., Versmann, A. (2011) Supporting environmentally sound decisions for waste management with LCT and LCA. *International Journal of Life Cycle Assessment*, 16(9): 937–939.

Margerum, R.D. (1999) Integrated environmental management: The foundations for successful practice. *Environmental Management*, 24(2): 151–166.

Martinsuo, M. (2009) Teaching the fuzzy front end of innovation: Experimenting with team learning and cross-organizational integration. *Creativity and Innovation Management*, 18(3): 147–159.

Mathisen, G.E., Einarsen, S., Jørstad, K., Brønnick, K.S. (2004) Climate for work group creativity and innovation: Norwegian validation of the team climate inventory (TCI). *Scandinavian Journal of Psychology*, 45(5): 383–392.

Mathisen, G.E., Torsheim, T. (2006) The team-level model of climate for innovation: A two-level confirmatory factor analysis. *Journal of Occupational & Organizational Psychology*, 79(1): 23–35.

Meadows, D. (1972) *The Limits to Growth, a Global Challenge: A Report for the Club of Rome Project on the Predicament of Mankind.* New York: Universe Books, p. 205.

Miozzo, M., Dewick, P. (2002) Building competitive advantage: Innovation and corporate governance in European construction. *Research Policy*, 31(6): 989–1008.

Mitropoulos, P., Tatum, C.B. (2000) Forces driving adoption of new information technologies. *Journal of Construction Engineering and Management*, 126(5): 340–348.

Mumford, M.D., Licuanan, B. (2004) Leading for innovation: Conclusions, issues, and directions. *Leadership Quarterly*, 15(1): 163–172.

Murphy, S.E., Ensher, E.A. (2008) A qualitative analysis of charismatic leadership in creative teams: The case of television directors. *Leadership Quarterly*, 19(3): 335–352.

Nameroff, T.J., Garant, R.J., Albert, M.B. (2004) Adoption of green chemistry: An analysis based on US patents. *Research Policy*, 33(6–7): 959–974.

Newell, S., Goussevskaia, A., Swan, J., Bresnen, M., Obembe, A. (2008) Interdependencies in complex project ecologies: The case of biomedical innovation. *Long Range Planning*, 41(1): 33–54.

Nieto, M.J., Santamaría, L. (2007) The importance of diverse collaborative networks for the novelty of product innovation. *Technovation*, 27(6–7): 367–377.

Orihata, M., Watanabe, C. (2000) The interaction between product concept and institutional inducement: A new driver of product innovation. *Technovation*, 20(1): 11–23.

Ozaki, R. Sevastyanova, K. (2011) Going hybrid: An analysis of consumer purchase motivations. *Energy Policy*, 39(5): 2217–2228.

Panizzolo, R. (1998) Managing innovation in SMEs: A multiple case analysis of the adoption and implementation of product and process design technologies. *Small Business Economics*, 11(1): 25–42.

Paramanathan, S., Farrukh, C., Phaal, R., Probert, D. (2004) Implementing industrial sustainability: The research issues in technology management. *R&D Management*, 34(5): 527–537.

Parrish, B.D. (2010) Sustainability-driven entrepreneurship: Principles of organization design. *Journal of Business Venturing*, 25(5): 510–523.

Paulsen, N., Maldonado, D., Callan, V.J., Ayoko, O. (2009) Charismatic leadership, change and innovation in an R&D organization. *Journal of Organizational Change*, 22(5): 511–523.

Peltier, N.P., Ashford, N.A. (1998) Assessing and rationalizing the management of a portfolio of clean technologies: Experience from a French environmental fund and a World Bank Cleaner Production demonstration project in China. *Journal of Cleaner Production*, 6(2): 111–117.

Plambeck, E.L., Taylor, T.A. (2007) Implications of breach remedy and renegotiation design for innovation and capacity. *Management Science*, 53(12): 1859–1871.

Prencipe, A., Tell, F. (2001) Inter-project learning: Processes and outcomes of knowledge codification in project-based firms. *Research Policy*, 30(9): 1373–1394.

Prothero, A., McDonagh, P., Dobscha, S. (2010) Is green the new black? Reflections on a green commodity discourse. *Journal of Macromarketing*, 30(2): 147–159.

Rampersad, G., Quester, P., Troshani, I. (2010) Managing innovation networks: Exploratory evidence from ICT, biotechnology and nanotechnology networks. *Industrial Marketing Management*, 39(5): 793–805.

Reijnders, L., Huijbregts, M.A.J. (2000) Tools for the environmental evaluation and improvement of buildings. *Milieu: Journal of Environmental Sciences*, 15(2): 89–96.

Ring, P.S., Van de Ven, A.H. (1994) Developmental processes of cooperative inter-organizational relationships. *Academy of Management Review*, 19(1): 90–118.

Ritter, T., Gemünden, H.G. (2003) Network competence: Its impact on innovation success and its antecedents. *Journal of Business Research*, 56(9): 745–755.

Roeloffzen, L. (2010) *The Influence of the Sustainability Purchase Policy on Enterprises within the Construction Industry*. M.Sc. thesis VU University Amsterdam.

Rosenberg, W. (2004) Making a profit . . . and a difference: HP invents an organization to drive sustainability. *Journal of Organizational Excellence*, 23(3): 3–13.

Rothaermel, F.T., Hess, A.M. (2007) Building dynamic capabilities: Innovation driven by individual-, firm-, and network-level effects. *Organization Science*, 18(6): 898–921.

Rothwell, R. (1992) Industrial innovation and governmental regulation: Some lessons from the past. *Technovation*, 12(7): 447–458.

Rumelt, R.P. (1984) Towards a strategic theory of the firm. In: Lamb, R.B. (ed.) *Competitive Strategic Management*. Englewood Cliffs: Prentice-Hall, pp. 566–570.

Scarbrough, H., Swan, J., Laurent, S., Bresnen, M., Edelman, L., Newell, S. (2004) Project-based learning and the role of learning boundaries. *Organization Studies*, 25(9): 1579–1600.

Schaltegger, S., Wagner, M. (2011) Sustainable entrepreneurship and sustainability innovation: Categories and interactions. *Business Strategy and the Environment*, 20(4): 222–237.

Schumpeter, J.A. (1934) *The Theory of Economic Development: An Inquiry into Profits, Capital, Credit, Interest, and the Business Cycle*. Cambridge Mass.: Harvard University Press, p. 255.

Seaden, G., Manseau, A. (2001) Public policy and construction innovation. *Building Research & Information*, 29(3): 182–196.

Sha, K., Deng, X., Cui, C. (2000) Sustainable construction in China: Status quo and trends. *Building Research & Information*, 28(1): 59–66.

Shen, L., Tam, V.W.Y., Tam, L., Ji, Y. (2010) Project feasibility study: The key to successful implementation of sustainable and socially responsible construction management practice. *Journal of Cleaner Production*, 18(3): 254–259.

Shepherd, D.A., Patzelt, H. (2010) The new field of sustainable entrepreneurship: Studying entrepreneurial action linking "what is to be sustained" with "what is to be developed." *Entrepreneurship: Theory and Practice*, 35(1): 137–163.

Sheth, J.N., Sethia, N.K., Srinivas, S. (2011) Mindful consumption: A customer-centric approach to sustainability. *Journal of the Academy of Marketing Science*, 39(1): 21–39.

Shipton, H., West, M., Parkes, C., Dawson, J., Patterson, M. (2006) When promoting positive feelings pays: Aggregate job satisfaction, work design features, and innovation in manufacturing organizations. *European Journal of Work and Organizational Psychology*, 15(4): 404–430.

Shrivastava, P. (1995) The role of corporations in achieving ecological sustainability. *Academy of Management Review*, 20(4): 936–960.

Sigurdson, J., Cheng, A.L.P. (2001) New technological links between national innovation systems and corporations. *International Journal of Technology Management*, 22(5–6): 417–434.

Sim, E.W., Griffin, A., Price, R.L., Vojak, B.A. (2007) Exploring differences between inventors, champions, implementers and innovators in creating and developing new products in large, mature firms. *Creativity and Innovation Management*, 16(4): 422–436.

Smith, A., Stirling, A., Berkhout, F. (2005) The governance of sustainable sociotechnical transitions. *Research Policy*, 34(10): 1491–1510.

Soosay, C.A. (2005) An empirical study of individual competencies in distribution centres to enable continuous innovation. *Creativity and Innovation Management*, 14(3): 299–310.

Spithoven, A., Clarysse, B., Knockaert, M. (2010) Building absorptive capacity to organise inbound open innovation in traditional industries. *Technovation*, 30(2): 130–141.

Starik, M., Rands, G.P. (1995) Weaving an integrated web: Multilevel and multisystem perspectives of ecologically sustainable organizations. *Academy of Management Review*, 20(4): 908–935.

Steurer, R., Konrad, A. (2009) Business-society relations in Central-Eastern and Western Europe: How those who lead in sustainability reporting bridge the gap in corporate (social) responsibility. *Scandinavian Journal of Management*, 25(1): 23–36.

Surie, G., Ashley, A. (2007) Integrating pragmatism and ethics in entrepreneurial leadership for sustainable value creation. *Journal of Business Ethics*, 81(1): 235–246.

Thorgren, S., Wincent, J., Örtqvist, D. (2009) Designing interorganizational networks of innovation: An empirical examination of network configuration, formation and governance. *Journal of Engineering and Technology Management*, 26(3): 148–166.

Toole, T.M. (1998) Uncertainty and home builders' adoption of technological innovations. *Journal of Construction Engineering and Management*, 124(4): 323–332.

Tsoutsos, T.D., Stamboulis, Y.A. (2005) The sustainable diffusion of renewable energy technologies as an example of an industry-focused policy. *Technovation*, 25(7): 753–762.

UNCED (1992) *Agenda 21*, Rio de Janeiro, pp. 6–11.

Van Aken, J.E. (2005) Management research as a design science: Articulating the research products of mode 2 knowledge production in management. *British Journal of Management*, 16(1): 19–36.

Van der Wiel, A. (2010) *An Explorative Study on Waste Reduction Using Reverse Logistics within the Cradle-to-Cradle Context*. M.Sc. thesis VU University Amsterdam.

Van der Wiel, A., Bossink, B.A.G., Masurel, E. (2012) Reverse logistics for waste reduction in cradle-to-cradle-oriented firms: Waste management strategies in the Dutch metal industry. *International Journal of Technology Management*, 60(1–2): 96–113.

Van de Vrande, V., De Jong, J.P.J., Vanhaverbeke, W., De Rochemont, M. (2009) Open innovation in SMEs: Trends, motives and management challenges. *Technovation*, 29(6–7): 423–437.

Verloop, J.H. (2008) *Environmental Policy Planning and the Stimulation of Environmental Sustainable Innovations*. M.Sc. thesis VU University Amsterdam.

Veshosky, D. (1998) Managing innovation information in engineering and construction firms. *Journal of Management in Engineering*, 14(1): 58–66.

Voegtlin, C., Patzer, M., Scherer, A.G. (2012) Responsible leadership in global business: A new approach to leadership and its multi-level outcomes. *Journal of Business Ethics*, 105(1): 1–16.

Von Malmborg, F. (2003) Conditions for regional public-private partnerships for sustainable development—Swedish perspectives. *European Environment*, 13(3): 133–149.

Von Zedtwitz, M., Gassmann, O. (2002). Market versus technology drive in R&D internationalization: Four different patterns of managing research and development. *Research Policy*, 31(4): 569–588.

Vuola, O., Hameri, A.P. (2006) Mutually benefiting joint innovation process between industry and big-science. *Technovation*, 26(1): 3–12.

Wagner, M., Llerena, P. (2011) Eco-innovation through integration, regulation and cooperation: Comparative insights from case studies in three manufacturing sectors. *Industry and Innovation*, 18(8): 747–765.

Waldman, D.A., Galvin, B.M. (2008) Alternative perspectives of responsible leadership. *Organizational Dynamics*, 37(4): 327–341.

Whyte, J., Ewenstein, B., Hales, M., Tidd, J. (2008) Visualizing knowledge in project-based work. *Long Range Planning*, 41(1): 74–92.

Williams, L.K., McGuire, S.J. (2010) Economic creativity and innovation implementation: The entrepreneurial drivers of growth? Evidence from 63 countries. *Small Business Economics*, 34(4): 391–412.

Wu, W.-Y., Chang, M.-L., Chen, C.-W. (2008) Promoting innovation through the accumulation of intellectual capital, social capital, and entrepreneurial orientation. *R&D Management*, 38(3): 265–277.

York, J.G., Venkataraman, S. (2010) The entrepreneur-environment nexus: Uncertainty, innovation, and allocation. *Journal of Business Venturing*, 25(5): 449–463.

Index

178   *Index*

For Product Safety Concerns and Information please contact our EU
representative GPSR@taylorandfrancis.com
Taylor & Francis Verlag GmbH, Kaufingerstraße 24, 80331 München, Germany

www.ingramcontent.com/pod-product-compliance
Ingram Content Group UK Ltd.
Pitfield, Milton Keynes, MK11 3LW, UK
UKHW021608240425
457818UK00018B/451